A{{DVANCE}} P{{RAISE}} for *About Faces: Expressions of Alzheimer's and Dementia:*

"Wow! I found myself swept into special, intimate moments of lives having much to teach us. A book of emotions and a lifetime of wisdom, Hulett's words captures Alzheimer's perfectly!

—D{{ALE}} C. C{{ARTER}}, A{{UTHOR}}
Transitioning Your Aging Parent: A 5-step Guide through Crisis & Change

"Heart-wrenching and heart-warming, this book drew me in, making it impossible to put down. The author's understanding of raw emotions when dealing with memory disease is apparent, and his book is a must read for anyone going through the challenges."

—B{{ARBARA}} S{{TEWART}}

"There are great lessons for all of us in this book—to live each day and cherish your time and opportunities with each other in the moments. Well done from a completely different angle!"

—M{{ALOU}} V{{AN}} E{{IJK}}

"A powerful read! Heart-breaking, but also inspiring! Hulett's book puts a human face on a devastating disease . . ."

—J.H.

"Hulett's book is the Alzheimer's and dementia reality, and I related to the families because my mother had dementia. It's also a valuable resource for families and caregivers as they walk their own paths . . . there's no doubt Hulett's book will help!"

—*Cheryl Bastyr*

About Faces:

Expressions of Alzheimer's
and Dementia

ABOUT FACES:
EXPRESSIONS OF ALZHEIMER'S
and DEMENTIA

TAYLOR HULETT

Hulett Media
Denver, CO

DEDICATION

For Cheryl . . .

EILEEN TINKER

Eileen

Eileen looked at her son, delight twinkling in her eyes. "This is where I feel as if I don't have a care in the world— do you feel it?" She glanced at the lake's shore, then back at the man who was her pride and joy. "Do you?" Her voice was barely a whisper.

"Yes, Mom. I feel it . . ."

She didn't notice three steps leading to the cabin's porch were splintered, worn, and in need of replacing—or, the railing's tipping precariously on the south side. None of that mattered as he watched tears trace her cheeks down to her chin. To her?

Time meant nothing.

Then, she turned, as if trying to remember. "I always loved the leaves in Fall . . ."

Moments later, Brian turned the key in the lock, then stepped aside as he held the door. "It's going to be a little dusty!"

Stepping across the threshold, the scent of times long passed tickled her nose as she immediately focused on a small painting propped against the wall on the fireplace mantle. "Did I do that," she asked, searching her memory banks.

"Indeed, you did! It's always been my favorite . . ." He watched as his mother inched closer, eyes squinting to see the finest detail.

Then, without word, she scanned the small cabin's main room and kitchen. On a rustic oak end table was a picture of the family taken years prior—when life was as it should be—and, Brian thought he noticed a fleeting flicker of recognition.

But, on second look . . .

While she took a quick rest, he tidied up, making the cabin as pleasant as possible. Her spontaneous request to return to her roots allowed him no time to make appropriate arrangements, so he had to make do with the little he had—a bottle of Windex, and a rag.

Then, it was a quick supper of bacon and eggs, afterward settling into leather chairs in front of the fireplace—the air was on the cusp of a fall chill, and Brian knew his mom would enjoy it.

Tummies finally full, they sat, his hand cradling hers as twilight seeped in the windows, its chill a portend of what was to come. "Do you remember when Stacy and I skipped rocks at the water's edge, Mom?" He chuckled, recalling his sister never did quite get the hang of it. "I remember you told her not to give it a second thought—whether she could skip a stone didn't make a lick of difference!"

Brian glanced at Eileen, the rise and fall of her chest soft with each breath. He knew the trip would be tiring for her and, if he were to be honest, he tried to talk her out of it. Since diagnosed with Alzheimer's in 2007, her decline was noticeable, but not in need of a plan. But, by the time the decade turned, in a private meeting, he and his sister discussed what would be best, both agreeing she needed round-the-clock care—but, what that entailed, neither were quite sure.

But, no matter what the future held, there was one thing Brian knew—it was the last time his mom would remember the place of his childhood. Where she painted.

Where she dared to create.

Stacy stared at her coffee cup, her throat choked with emotion until, finally, she focused on her brother. "The bottom line is we can't afford it anymore . . ." As hard as she tried to restrain her tears, the dam broke. "I don't know what to do . . ."

"I know. I know . . ." Then, in silence, he allowed his sister to deal with her grief, knowing he was there for her, if needed.

"Do you have any ideas," she finally asked.

Brian nodded. "Well—I think we have to move her to Colorado. You know I've been working with Applewood Our House . . ."

Stacy stared at him. "Are you serious?"

"What choice do we have? She needs round-the-clock care, and having someone come in is draining us!" He paused, hoping she would offer a glimmer of acceptance. "Besides, I'm going to be there—it won't be as if she's totally alone. She'll meet people from day one . . ."

"I can look for a place here . . ."

"You know New York is too expensive . . ."

"That's true, but maybe I can find a place we can afford . . ."

"Well, okay. But, it has to be quick—both of us know she's deteriorating quickly—a hell of a lot faster than at the beginning."

Stacy didn't say anything as sorrow began to etch fine lines in her face within grief's secrecy.

Brian reached for her hand across the small, kitchen table, squeezing it gently. "We know the prognosis—all I want is for Mom to live her last years with dignity. And, grace . . ."

It was then their lives shattered.

After a month, it was clear New York was out. It wasn't that Stacy didn't try, but the emotional toll it took on her thwarted a full-on, targeted search. They agreed she would have four weeks to find something suitable—but, by the third week and although it was unspoken, both knew the ultimate decision.

Prior to his mother's illness, Brian worked on a few Applewood Our House homes during their construction phases, and he had a good feeling about the organization's work—it was getting Eileen into one of them that was the crapshoot. Even though her Alzheimer's was beginning to progress quicker, Brian and Stacy knew she would be well aware of her freedom being stripped, and no longer would she have familiarity of her home—her sanctuary. Memories of raising her children would fade, and connections she enjoyed for decades would wither.

Working on Applewood's homes, however, didn't prepare Brian for what was to come. He hadn't a clue of how difficult it would be to watch his mom drift to a place he didn't recognize.

Not one clue.

Getting Eileen to Colorado had to be based on secrecy, something that didn't sit well with either of them. They agonized over clandestine plans, recognizing the need to enlist the help of one of Brian's friends if they were to succeed. After much discussion, all three agreed his friend would pick up Stacy, Eileen, and him at the airport, and head directly for Applewood Our House.

As with all Applewood homes, there was an intake process, and it was then Eileen began to understand something wasn't right. Freedom?

Gone.

She sat quietly as Brian and Stacy answered the woman's questions, her eyes scanning the room. Unease mounted as a tiny nugget of truth lodged in her brain, and she turned to Brian, her eyes shiny with tears. "I don't understand . . ."

"Mom . . ."

"You're leaving me here?"

"Mom . . ."

As realization took root, fear and anxiety dug in, clutching her heart—and, for the first time, Brian wished he could lie to her. How he would have loved to tell her everything was just fine—seeing a look of peace on her face would have been reward enough. But, he couldn't—it wasn't how he was raised.

So, on that lonely night in June, Eileen Tinker's life changed—most likely, for the last time.

Stacy allowed tears to spill when she turned to leave her mom's room, wondering if she would see her again. Unfortunately, Alzheimer's wasn't fond of a definitive time frame, and her family's lives could change with little warning. Of course, she trusted her brother to take care of her, but that was little solace as she crossed the threshold.

"Stacy?" Eileen's voice was small and timid as she watched her daughter go. "Stacy?"

But, Stacy didn't look back—she couldn't. If she did, she knew her heart and soul would fracture, and it was a memory she didn't want for eternal time.

The intake coordinator told them it would take time for Eileen to adjust, and she was right. Of course, Brian visited regularly, but he knew it didn't take the place of what his mother knew and loved before Alzheimer's stole her life. At times, mercurial behavior became a concern, but they remembered the intake coordinator's words. "Sometime, between the fifth and sixth month," she advised, "a peace will settle over her, and she'll be different." Still, she was, at times, incorrigible and inconsolable, not understanding her situation. It was during those times, Brian wished he could lie—but, again, it wasn't his nature. She taught him to be forthright and honest, and he figured she deserved to be treated with respect fueled by the truth.

"I can't stand it when she asks about Dad," Brian confided to Stacy during a late-evening call. "When she does, she sinks into sadness and depression . . ."

"Does she realize he passed?"

"Not until I tell her—and, I've told her the same thing over and over. I'm finally to the point I *have* to lie—if I tell her the truth, it's as if she gets stuck in some sort of loop, and it causes nothing but turmoil."

Stacy was quiet for a moment, not only thinking of her mother, but what her brother was enduring, as well. "You know I'd be there if I could," she commented, her voice laced with sadness.

"I know . . .

CHAPTER TWO

COPING

There comes a time in everyone's life when ultimate truth transcends perspective and reality. Memories fade to a secret, mental compartment, only to surface when the soul needs, submerging again amidst efforts to merely cope— often in vain.

Brian and Stacy were, in many ways, on the sidelines during their mother's mental regression as she battled with herself, both suffering in the process. They couldn't help remember times when life was sweet, and neither of them had a care—it was in those memories, they recalled Eileen's love for flowers and gardening. "It's the delicate nature of life," she once told them, "that creates strength in all things."

As is often the case with brothers and sisters, Brian and Stacy were different personalities. Always ready to discover and explore, Brian was the kid who wound up in trouble, often grounded for his zeal when it came to trying new things. Stacy, however, preferred to think before leaping into something of which she knew nothing, many times landing her in the position of the 'level-headed' child. Did Brian care?

Not really.

He was perfectly fine doing things that would get him dirty, rip his jeans, or slip slivers into his fingers. The truth? He was a loud kid. Obnoxious? Not quite. Unfortunately, though, his zest for life was, many times, a source of consternation for Eileen, who was quiet. Thoughtful. Reserved.

"You're grounded from four o'clock today until four o'clock next Friday," she would say, "and, you can't come out of your room except for school and chores . . ."

That also meant no music, television, or phone.

Brian, of course, pleaded his case, always implementing a well-thought out defense. "There are a million ways to do things, Mom!"

Although admiring her son's feisty, yet indefensible argument, it fell on deaf ears. "No—there's one way to do things. Mine!"

Clearly, Eileen's decisions had clout, and Brian got to know his room pretty well.

The interesting thing was Brian didn't mind conflict, often knowing he would be in for a little alone time. Stacy? Not so much—she preferred to stay in her mother's good graces. Still, for all of their differences in personality, they managed to find a way to deal with Eileen's illness and eventual passing together, yet in their own, individual way.

The worst time of year?

Christmas.

"Do you remember playing games, and eating Peanut M&Ms at the cabin," Brian asked his sister when she visited during Eileen's first Christmas at Applewood Our House.

"How could I forget?" Stacy propped up her feet on Brian's coffee table—it was good to be with family during the holidays, and she and Brian needed the connection. "Mom always made Christmas a piece of art . . ." She paused, recalling favorite times at the cabin, as well as Christmases at home. Between family and friends, there was always something going on, their home filled with singing and laughter.

That Christmas?

There wasn't much joy to go around.

The sting of Eileen's no longer being able to care for herself was still fresh, yet they were becoming accustomed to her increasing memory lapses.

"Do you think she remembers those days?"

Brian shook his head. "I doubt it, but I don't know . . ."

Stacy focused on her brother. "What's hardest for you? About mom's illness, I mean . . ."

Brian stared at fading, flickering flames in the fireplace. "The questions . . ."

"What questions?"

"You know—Mom was always a great talker, and she asked a million questions."

"For someone who's quiet most of the time, when she opens her mouth, everybody listens. I think asking questions was one of her strengths . . ."

"Agreed—but, haven't you noticed all of that's changed? She doesn't ask questions, anymore . . ." Brian paused, a lump in his throat staking its claim. "And, the truth is we stopped asking questions, too . . ."

Silence.

"We completely changed the way we are around her . . ."

"I never thought of it that way . . ."

Both were silent, one thing plaguing their thoughts. "You know," Stacy finally commented, "we could be in the same boat."

"Don't think I haven't thought about it—with grandparents on both sides having Alzheimer's, it makes me wonder about my future." Brian glanced at his sister. "Your's, too . . ."

"I suppose, after all of this ends, we should sit down and make a plan for that possible eventuality—as much as I hate thinking about it. I admit, it would be a whole lot easier to go through life with our heads stuck in the sand . . ."

"What scares me is what we're going through now . . . our families might experience the same grief we are."

Stacy shifted as one of her legs started to go to sleep. "I know—the thought takes me to a place I don't want to go. Let's face it—you and I are getting older. When it started with Mom, it inched forward—then, wham! She doesn't remember stuff we tell her . . ."

Brian sighed, his feet joining his sister's on the coffee table. "I can't imagine losing the ability to communicate . . ."

"Do you ever wonder what she thinks?"

"All the time—she told me once if she had any guts, she'd off herself . . ."

"What?"

"True story—then, she said, 'But, I don't have any guts, so you're stuck with me!'"

Neither said anything, until Stacy busted a huge laugh. "That sounds exactly like her!"

So, that evening as they sat on the couch with feet propped on the furniture, both came to terms with what might be their path, understanding they may be witnessing their own final years.

Neither had much to say.

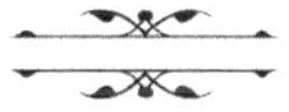

The second year was hell.

After the New Year, Stacy always kept in touch with Brian, but, as time crept forward, there really wasn't reason to visit. Eileen's moments of lucidity were becoming more infrequent, leaving the family to wonder if there were anything more to say—

it was a situation no one liked, yet they had to accept Eileen's life circling back to infancy.

Family was Brian's and Stacy's rock, spouses and children understanding and accommodating when emotions teetered on the edge of losing it. Standing beside those they love, family was always waiting in the wings to pick up the pieces if Eileen's Alzheimer's got the best of them.

But, there does come a time, I suppose, when life takes on a tinge of shaded reality. Brian's work was thriving, and Stacy had a professional counseling practice taking up much of her time. Not only that, Stacy lived nearly sixteen hundred miles from Denver—hopping on a plane whenever she wanted was easier said than done.

That, of course, left Brian in the position of straightening his shoulders to carry any immediate burden that may arise. Throughout the year, there were certain situations requiring his attention, but, for the most part, life consisted of work, family, and watching Eileen grapple with her illness—the latter clutching his heart as her life remained in limbo.

At the onset of Eileen's diagnosis, there wasn't much thought about how difficult it would be on Eileen's grandchildren. Brian and Stacy soon found out, however, their grandmother's decline affected them, as well. Perhaps not understanding the intricacies of her illness, they wanted to see her when they could, and Brian often wondered if watching her regression would have an adverse effect as they matured. They wouldn't know until the children were older, but, he and his wife did everything they could to negate such a possibility. Discussions filled with tears helped them cope, yet he couldn't help wondering what they would do when their hearts broke.

Brian was particularly concerned about his fourteen-year-old adopted daughter—the first years of her life were emotionally scarring, and he didn't want to heap anything onto her lap.

The backstory?

Well—some kids, as you know, are born into families who love and adore them—then, there are those who are abused and neglected with little regard for their lives.

Meet Zion—a lovely, deaf, young lady from China.

When Brian and his wife heard of her situation at noon on a Monday, Zion was living with them by dinnertime on Tuesday. As you might imagine, there were FBI and Interpol checks to make certain they were suitable adoptive parents and, somehow, everything fell into place. But, there was one, difficult issue . . .

Communication.

With little more than twenty-four hours notice before Zion came into their lives, it was a good bet no one knew sign language. That, however, wasn't an obstacle—over the course of her first six months with them, they learned and, slowly, Zion began to emerge from her shell, finally communicating. Now twenty-two, she deals with life well, yet there are deep, scarring emotional issues.

Unfortunately, Eileen couldn't be there to help, her second year at Applewood completely opposite of the first—that year was filled with anger, wanting to get out, and trying to get out. A physical woman, she took it out on the caregivers, seething with anger.

Then, a sudden sense of peace.

"She doesn't have any idea of what's happening," Brian informed Stacy during a late-night call. "That's the problem—she doesn't understand."

He listened as Stacy tried to choke back tears. "Is she still afraid?"

"I don't think so—it's weird. I remember someone at Applewood telling me that would happen, and we noticed it around the end of her first year. At least, I did . . ."

"Me, too—especially when I was there for Christmas."

"Now . . . it's even more so."

"How is she getting along with the caregivers?"

Brian chuckled, although he knew he shouldn't. "She hates them—especially when one leaves, and she has to break in someone new!"

"I can see it now!" Stacy paused. "What does she say?"

"She says she doesn't like them—many times!"

A long silence.

"I try to be honest and upfront with her," Brian continued, "but, it's dumb because all that does is provoke turmoil. Every time I'm honest, she asks about Dad . . ."

"What do you say?"

"I tell her he died . . ."

"And?"

"She gets sad all of a sudden . . ."

For the next few minutes they chatted, finally ending with their customary, 'I love you.' Brian clicked off, thinking about how much their lives changed when his mom was diagnosed.

That was when he wished he would have started lying to her sooner.

Years passed. The second year tumbled into Eileen's third, and that was the course until her fifth year at Applewood Our House—longer than most, leaving Brian and Stacy to wonder if that were a good thing. Of course, it was—the more time they had with their mother, the more precious each minute. And, as Eileen slowly drifted to a world her children couldn't recognize, they thought more about the past than the future.

Memories were always with them, available to hold close when needed, then recede when feeling as if they had things under control. For Brian and Stacy there were more moments of wonderful days passed than there were of Eileen's illness, guiding them through difficult times.

Then, year five.

Brian still built additional Applewood Our House homes, his work and personal life forever bonded by Eileen's strength as she continued to meld into a world only she knew. Stacy visited when she could, distance being the only thing keeping her from her mother.

"We're nearing the end of our journey," Brian confided to his sister in one of their customary, late-night phone conversations. "As much as I know the outcome, there's a part of me wanting to refuse to accept it . . ."

Stacy was quiet, thinking about what few would voice. "I know—I feel the same way. But, things are changing, and we have to accept our time with her is limited."

"I get it. But, I'm not so sure I know how to do that . . ."

"Neither do I, but I'm sure I'll learn . . ."

CHAPTER THREE

ACCEPTANCE

Acceptance—a tricky thing for some. Most, probably. Some say it takes time, while others tout total acceptance of life's situations whether they mean it or not. For Brian and Stacy, it was something with which they grappled for the better part of a year. Yes, there was acceptance when Eileen moved to Applewood Our House—but, it wasn't the same. Being embroiled in the chaos of making decisions, the actual move, and getting their mother settled masked reality, it wasn't until the last couple of years did they give themselves permission to grieve before—not only after— her passing.

You know how, sometimes, you forget what day it is? Well, for Eileen, as her disease progressed, it were as if she were caught in a cycle. "Where's Ted," she'd ask, as if expecting him to walk in the door any minute, completely unaware her husband passed fifteen or sixteen years prior. Brian and Stacy found her question tough to answer because she'd ask them the same thing the following day. Week. Month.

Brian's answer was always the same. "He's on a trip, Mom—he'll be back in a week, or two." Although he knew it was a blatant lie, it didn't matter—his response was one giving his mother peace instead of turmoil. It helped her handle the here and now because Eileen knew things for only a finite period of time—maybe, a minute—then, she'd ask the question again. Toward the end of her life, she remembered for only two or three seconds, tops.

Her son called it a 'loop.'

As her illness progressed, someone new in her life might say, "Hi! My name is . . ." Then, a few seconds later, Eileen would ask, "What's your name?" The sad fact was Eileen simply couldn't process information, anymore.

You can imagine how difficult it was on Brian, as well as Stacy when she visited. It was like learning to negotiate with his parent and, in some ways, it felt as if he were betraying her when he wasn't being honest.

As Eileen declined, dealing with her was like dealing with a small child—laughter and distraction worked well. When visiting his mom, Brian would often say, "Hey, Mom! Look over here . . ." when she forgot what she was doing.

Caregivers, he found out, were really good at it—but, family members? Not so much. So, what better way to learn than through observation? He watched them, learned what to do and say, then implemented their techniques. "It's almost like family training from caregivers," he told Stacy on the phone.

She sniffled. "This is the hardest thing I've ever gone through—and, I can't imagine what it's like for you. You're dealing with it constantly . . ."

"I just want her to be at peace . . ." There was no mistaking tears in his voice.

So, as Eileen's memory deteriorated, life was difficult. But, the most important thing Brian wanted for his mom?

Dignity.

It was something staff recognized and wanted to provide, as well. Brian and Stacy appreciated their ability to be vibrant and available, and it were as if they were living life with Eileen, not simply caring for her. It was all about the daily things, and great conversations that made her feel safe and secure.

Still, even with all the support and help from family and caregivers, one thought stuck with Brian each day . . .

It's so unfair.

As uncomfortable as it was to admit, Brian was angry. His mother shouldn't be in a position such as hers, and he shouldn't be in a position to be her parent—which, in many ways, was exactly what was happening.

But, in his heart, he knew it was silly to be angry—calling the entire situation unfair—for doing so only signified remnants of raw emotion. He felt ridiculous for having such thoughts, no matter how understandable. In his private moments, the thought of his mom not being at his side, traveling life, was difficult to bear—after all, he was only thirty years old when Eileen was diagnosed, and thirty-seven when her conditioned worsened.

Pretty young.

CHAPTER FOUR

CELEBRATION OF LIFE

Then, hospice.

Brian appreciated the excellent hospice care taking place at Applewood Our House—not having to move his mom provided great comfort during such an emotional time not only for Eileen, but for him, as well.

As end of life neared, he went into his mom's room, wanting to make sure he had time with her. "How do you really know," he asked, watching the hospice caregiver tend to Eileen.

"We don't. Your mom can go another hour, twenty-four hours, or three days . . ."

He didn't say anything as he held her hand—but, he knew.

So, there they sat—talking, and Eileen passed twenty-six minutes later. He still held her hand, not telling anyone for a half hour, or so—he couldn't. Brian wanted more time—more time to love her, more time to listen to her laugh.

More time for her to love him.

When it was time, he contacted hospice. They took it from there, making phone calls within the network. Caregivers often worked at all of Applewood's homes, and they were considered family. It didn't take long for word to travel the grapevine about Eileen's passing. Suddenly, calls poured in, and those who knew her best began arriving to celebrate her life. Everyone was crying, of course, and it was an exceptional moment—Brian could actually feel the impact his mom had on everyone there. *Even battling Alzheimer's, Mom, you were a force . . .*

You know, it's sad—many think when one is struggling to endure the hardships of Alzheimer's, the person no longer contributes—but, that isn't true. They contribute to filling the lives of those working with them. And, let's face it—to choose working with memory care residents—well, perhaps it's a choice.

Perhaps it's a calling.

As Brian drove home that evening, he thought about the beginning of Eileen's illness so many years ago. That was when he really paid attention to genetics—Alzheimer's was in his family, and it was something he couldn't dismiss. Initially, his mom's symptoms were nothing more than a little fogginess— then, it burrowed in, inching forward. Questions asked, and re-asked. Not only once—but, fifteen or twenty times.

He thought about the years from beginning to end, and the anger he felt—the frustration—knowing all of it was worth it.

He hoped she knew he would always be with her.

Do you remember Cape Cod, Mom? When you walked on the beach, loving every second of it?

He knew she did.

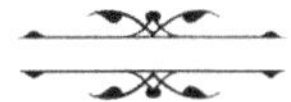

It's been a couple of years since Eileen's passing.

Brian's life returned to normal, pleased his kids had time with their grandmother. Her illness was difficult for them, and he could only surmise it was hard on Eileen during the years before her illness won—and, because it stretched on longer than most, it was an emotional roller coaster for everyone.

Most times, Brian thinks Alzheimer's will always win— but, he has hope. He learned he would do just about anything to help his mom have peaceful days before passing. "The whole thing was difficult," he told Stacy, many months later. "Things like taking her car away—and, moving her to a home where she would spend her remaining days. At times, I wasn't sure if I could handle it . . ."

"But, you did. We did. We handled it—and, Mom knows we were at her side."

"If I had to explain to anyone what it's like . . . well, I don't know if I can accurately describe it. I don't like telling anyone they're going to be sad, frustrated, and angry."

"I know . . ."

"Do you remember when we took her car? We had to tell her it wasn't safe for her to drive—do you remember what she did?"

"Yes! She stared at us for twenty minutes!"

Brian laughed aloud at the memory. "You know—as funny as it was, it was a brutal moment."

"We had a lot of brutal moments . . ."

"You're right about that . . ." He was quiet for a moment. "That we did . . ."

A few minutes later, they clicked off, leaving Brian to his thoughts. Conversations about Eileen always made him contemplative and, as he sat, he realized what he missed most.

His mom's art.

They were similar, he and Eileen—except his talent was within the performing arts, her's visual. She'd start a project at nine in the morning, and finish at four the following morning— refusing to stop, she wouldn't eat or sleep until it was complete.

So, one fall day, a young boy asked if she could draw Joe Montana. "Of course, I can," she said, promising she would do just that.

Twenty hours later? A seventeen-by-fourteen picture of Joe Montana with a football next to his head, and a logo in the corner. The truth was it could have sold—especially in San Francisco— but, she chose to give it to a twelve-year old boy who was moving through life with challenges.

That's how she rolled.

BILL CARTER

CHAPTER FIVE

Bill

ill Carter was the kind of guy who wanted to see the world—you know, experience life. Cultures. Things of which he knew nothing.

So, to him, it made perfect sense to join the military.

It was no surprise when he was accepted to the Naval Academy, finishing his schooling four years later at the height of the Vietnam war—a dangerous time for those who fought on the lines, as well as men and women serving behind the scenes.

It was then he met his wife, Dale, shortly after his Naval Academy graduation—she was a junior at a Virginia college—and, after discussing the pros and cons of naval life, being a military wife was okay with her. She planned on traveling, anyway, seeing the world, never intending to marry—but, when

Bill Carter waltzed into her life? Things changed. Before they knew it?

Hitched.

Military life worked for both of them for a while, but there was one thing standing at the ready to squirrel their plans—prejudice. The sixties were unpleasant times, soldiers returning from war often met with boos as they disembarked from their planes—or, spat upon as they walked by onlookers. There was little question the Vietnam war ignited the worst in people and, with such turbulent circumstances to consider, they finally decided to exit the military, both ready to live a civilian life. Yes, it was a difficult decision, but it was one they had to make.

With a background in operations analysis, pursuing an engineering career seemed the best bet. Bill always enjoyed doing things with his hands—gardening, and his ever-growing, thirty foot model train. It was during those years he eased into a life he enjoyed, his wife noticing how much he was like his father—a renaissance kind of guy, trying everything, and tasting life.

Then, kids. Three within twenty months—obviously, a set of twins in the mix. "We're outnumbered," he would often say with a smile, enjoying every bit of fatherhood. Still—it was a big change.

Finally settling in Indiana, it was there they stayed for thirty years, Bill changing jobs occasionally, finally landing his favorite position as a research and chemical engineer at the University of Notre Dame.

Life was good.

"Look at my new cabinets," he bragged as he led his wife through his brand new lab. "Walnut!"

She looked at him, her pride obvious. "They're beautiful!"

"Best thing I've ever had!"

She matched his grin. "And, just what is it you're going to do in here?"

"Oh, you know—build complex test equipment." He hesitated, scanning the lab. "Plus, we're working on a new class of refrigerants—energy efficient, and cost-effective." Of course, he never thought much about the complexities of his work. It was just something he loved to do—and, he did it until he was sixty-eight.

Then, a change.

"I think it's time," he commented to Dale one summer morning.

"Time for what?" She turned from piling plates into the dishwasher, giving him her complete attention.

"To do other things . . ."

Dale's eyebrows arched. "Retirement?"

Bill nodded. "I've had my run—now, it's time to move on."

She nodded, not quite knowing what to say. She knew it was the right decision, and it was one neither of them took lightly. Then, she grinned, resuming loading the dishwasher. "How exciting!"

Not long after, life shifted.

"Have you noticed changes," Dale's mother asked.

Her daughter recognized concern in her mom's voice. "Changes? In what?"

"Not what—who."

Dale stopped what she was doing, focusing on her mom intently. "What are you talking about?"

Her mother paused, uncertain if she should continue. Clearly, her daughter hadn't noticed a thing. "Bill . . ."

"Bill? What about him?" Her mom's answer was somewhat of a surprise because she was dying from cancer, Dale automatically assumed she was referring to herself. But, Bill? Never in a million years . . .

"I know you weren't paying attention, but, when everyone was together a few days ago, I noticed something . . ."

"You mean he's slowing down a bit?"

Her mom shook her head. "No—it's the way he walks. And, he's confused . . ."

Dale stared at her, tears starting to well. Of course, she noticed something—after all, she worked in a health facility as an administrator specializing in memory care. How could she not notice?

It was at that moment she recognized her denial.

It was a reality difficult to comprehend—Bill didn't have any family members with it. Even so, symptoms were unmistakable, and an undeniable fact.

Not long after, Dale and Bill had the difficult conversation that had to be, and getting him in with his primary physician became their number one goal—doing so, however, proved to be a ponderous process. The V.A. didn't want to speak with her because she hadn't filled out the proper forms—a process that took nearly a year to the time Bill walked in their doors. And, that's what was so difficult—not only for Bill, but for Dale, as well. She knew, without question, he had Lewy Body Dementia—she knew its symptoms inside out.

She also knew they were devastating.

"I know the outcome," she confided to her son, Chris, in tears. "I know what will be . . ."

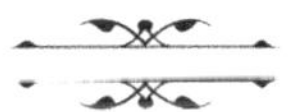

"We're going to send you to a neuropsychologist . . ." Bill's primary physician glanced at Bill, then at Dale. "Just for testing purposes . . ."

Naturally, they complied, and Bill spent hours enduring paper and pencil tests. When completed, the diagnosis was one they didn't expect. "He has mild, cognitive impairment," the doc told Dale.

Stunned, words failed her, but only for a moment. "He does not! It's beyond that—way beyond!"

The doctor wasn't sure how to respond. "Well," he finally advised, "that's beyond me . . ."

"Then, we need a referral . . ."

"Agreed. Mayo? Cleveland Clinic's also an option—both are strong in the brain disorder department . . ."

A few weeks later, Dale sat in the waiting room at Cleveland Clinic, waiting for her husband who was, again, enduring the testing procedure. Within a day or two, results turned out to be interesting—doctors discovered REM Sleep Disorder, which Dale knew was a component of Lewy Body Dementia. In fact, he'd been to doctors previously to test for sleep apnea, the results always negative. But, in her gut, Dale knew it was much more serious—and, when she learned of the REM Sleep Disorder diagnosis, things fell into place, no longer left to her own conjecture.

The love of her life had Lewy Body Dementia.

That was when Dale recognized their future. Her husband's disease was incurable, but, with medication, there was a possibility of slowing its progression—for her, their remaining days together were all about quality of life.

"Does he know what's going on," Dale's mother asked during a private conversation after learning of the diagnosis.

"Oh, yes—shortly after we got home, he began researching Lewy Body, and he's very clear his projected life expectancy is five to seven years . . ."

Her mother was quiet, thinking about the years ahead for Bill and her daughter. Her grandchildren. Struggling with cancer, her ability to help was somewhat depleted, but being there for them was top priority. "Of course, you know I'll do whatever I can . . ."

"I know, Mom. I know . . ."

"It's early, but do you have a plan?"

Dale didn't answer immediately, but, when she did, her voice was tinged with resignation. "Well, my work experience will help—we focus on building strengths, and talents. Bill loves trains, so I'll make sure he has that to keep his mind occupied— and, he also has a bit of artistic ability he inherited from his dad, I believe."

"That's good . . ."

"There are Alzheimer's and dementia services in South Bend—they have an adult day program. But, if it's anything like services we recommend at work, getting him in will be a challenge . . ."

"Why—don't they have enough room?"

"I doubt it's that—usually, they accept individuals who are much further along in the disease's progression."

As they talked, it was clear Dale's work with memory care would be a godsend. Her main concern was socialization—Bill was an introvert, and he was already beginning to withdraw. So, it was a grand day when they received word he was accepted! The organization started an 'early stage' program, and it was perfect—once a week, an art therapist worked with him, and they'd work on a project for about an hour and a half, coupled with lunch and social time with other program participants. Music was also important and, eventually, Bill compiled a playlist of his favorite music which he kept on his iPod.

Perhaps most touching was Bill's life story, created with the help of staff, and his wife. Dale provided photos and, after several weeks, he had a time line of family and friends he struggled to remember.

Still, it was a comfort.

During those difficult months of the early stages, Bill enjoyed the hands-on program—woodworking, in particular. Volunteers—older gentlemen who understood dementia, and its challenges—managed the shop. When working on projects, they'd have much of Bill's project precut, but that wasn't what Bill wanted.

"No, no, no! You're not doing it right," he'd argue, but always to no avail. The fact was there were things Bill couldn't do simply because they weren't safe. Even so, he stayed with it, often returning home with a project he claimed wasn't perfect, yet he and Dale kept it—others were sold, benefiting the Alzheimer's program.

But, there were still issues. The commute to the Cleveland Clinic took five hours, and traffic was always terrible. Not only that, they had to stay in a hotel, which proved difficult for Bill. So, all things considered and even though the program was wonderful, they made the shift to Rush Clinic outside of Chicago—only two hours from home.

As it turned out, the change was good for Bill. He connected with an excellent neurologist, immediately forging a positive relationship because she treated him as if he were normal.

The positive treatment environment proved a blessing to Dale, and it was during that time she realized her husband, most likely, had Parkinson's for nearly three years prior to his diagnosis. Doctors agreed, yet kept him on minimal medications, not treating him for Parkinson's until he absolutely needed it. "We have to be careful about interactions," the doctor told them.

"Interactions in what way," Dale asked, although she was certain she knew the answer.

"Medication reactions with the Lewy Body . . ."

So, as they tried to cope, Dale bounced between her husband's illness, as well as her mom's—the cancer was in advanced stages—prompting them to plan for end of life. Bill was lucky to be in respite care, allowing Dale a modicum of peace of mind.

But, she still worried.

Again, life shifted.

Dale's mom passed in 2015 and, in 2017, Bill's sister passed, as well.

"You can't keep doing this alone, Mom!" Chris flew in to help getting his dad to the funeral on Long Island, Bill's deterioration a considerable shock.

"I can handle it . . ."

"No! No you can't! You don't see it because you're so close to the situation, but Dad is declining. It's not going to be long before he's going to need care around the clock—and, you can't handle it without help!"

Dale eyed her son. "Are you saying I'm losing my objectivity?"

"Yes! That's exactly what I'm saying!"

Dale's eyes filled with tears, her mind grappling with the truth. "You're right," she finally admitted. "What do you suggest?"

"I think you should move to Denver—that way, I can help you."

"But, what about Seattle? Your sister lives there, and she can be a big help, too. I know she wants to . . ."

Chris reached for his mom's hand. "I know—it's a decision you'll have to make. Whether you choose Seattle or Denver, it will be better than staying here without a support system. Without help . . ."

So, after the funeral, Dale had a decision to make, and she did her due diligence, jotting the pros and cons of each city on a small tablet she always kept with her.

She chose Denver.

It was the perfect decision—well-known for it's incredible climate, she couldn't think of a place she'd rather be—or, a better place for Bill.

In April of 2017, the process of downsizing began, clearing their home of thirty years of clutter, as well as things they no longer needed. Of course, she couldn't tell Bill they were getting rid of anything—he had a basement full of stuff he cherished, and the thought of telling him he could no longer have it was an unbearable thought.

Time for little fibs . . .

Then, in September, it was time. Bill and Dale moved to Denver, even with Dale's knowing there was still much to figure out—things she had to get in place. But, eventually, everything worked out . . .

As things usually do.

CHAPTER SIX

CHANGES

*T*aking care of her husband was becoming more difficult, and the time finally came when it turned into a two-person endeavor. When Bill was up all night, she knew it was time to seek a facility where he could have appropriate care twenty-four seven.

Even so, Dale soldiered through her responsibilities without complaint, yet she looked forward to her upcoming college reunion in Virgina. It was clear she needed a break, but, before she could go, Dale needed to know her husband would be in good hands.

She began scouting facilities for two weeks of respite care for him, and finding a permanent facility wasn't on her mind—well, maybe it was, but she wasn't ready to go that route quite yet. All she needed was care for her husband for two weeks, then she'd be back at it.

A friend recommended a few places and Dale visited, finally winding up at Applewood Our House. Of course, Dale's having a career in memory care was a huge plus, providing her with the knowledge to ask appropriate and critical questions. "What type of training do you provide," she asked the Applewood intake coordinator.

"We train according to Teepa Snow—her strategies and philosophies."

That was all Dale needed to hear, and she knew she found the perfect facility for her husband. Just by walking in the door, she recognized the excellent training, as well as the culture her husband needed. At first blush, it was perfect—but, not really. The facility had space, but not on a temporary basis.

"I have a permanent space available," Sherrie told her, noticing the pain in Dale's eyes. "I'm sorry, but there just isn't anything for a temporary situation . . ."

Dale didn't speak for a moment, weighing her thoughts. "I don't think I'm ready for that . . ."

"I completely understand . . ."

Dale continued looking at options until Bill's palliative care social worker paid a visit a day or two later, assessing Bill's condition. It was then Dale recognized Bill was deteriorating, and he was beyond adult day care.

The social worker pulled her aside as they walked to the parking lot. "This isn't working for Bill, anymore," she advised.

It was exactly what Dale didn't want to hear, yet she knew she would. "Thank you for telling me . . ."

That moment?

Everything changed.

The following day, Dale got in touch with Sherrie at Applewood. "I'm ready," she said, tears in her eyes. "I can't keep him at home, anymore . . ."

It was a tough decision. Naturally, she explored other options, but none seemed viable. In-home care always posed a challenge, and Dale figured she didn't need that heaped on her plate—nor did Bill. It would only prolong certain eventuality.

Choice made.

Although it was a difficult decision, Dale went to her reunion after moving Bill in and, when she returned, she was thrilled to see he adjusted beautifully—it was, to him, home. His considering Applewood Our House home, of course, was based from his need for security and, although it was understandable, there was a pinprick of sadness when Dale fully realized she was no longer his home.

That meant restructuring her life.

Simple in thought, perhaps, but not so easy when it came to making changes. Involvement in her church's youth group offered a healthy distraction, as did support groups. A big plus was Bill's permanent placement in Applewood allowed her more time to spend with her granddaughter, as well as exploring Colorado.

Still, something was missing.

"I need to do something in a professional capacity," she told her daughter on the phone.

"Like what?"

"Oh, I don't know—I know I have a bunch of great experience in many things, thanks to my age. But, I don't think I want to go that route . . ."

"Well, whatever you decide, you have my support!"

With her children's blessing—not that she really needed it—it wasn't long before Dale knew she needed to give back. She understood what so many come to realize when faced with a life-altering situation—giving back is a critical element of moving forward. Friends were always calling for advice—especially those dealing with similar circumstances—and, there was a fulfilling satisfaction she truly enjoyed.

Bill, however, was still her main focus and, when his forty-fifth Navel Academy reunion came into play, Dale was hoping he could attend.

"I'm not talking about flying," she advised Bill's doctor. "But, do you think he's okay enough for me to drive him to Maryland?"

"I think so . . ."

So, armed with a wheelchair and walker provided by the V.A., in September of 2016, their journey began. Before making the trek, Dale contacted the alumnus in charge of making reunion arrangements, letting him know of their situation. "If we come," she said, "we'll need help . . ."

"Not to worry—we'll give you all the help you need."

As exciting as it was to think about Bill's having a bit of normalcy while reminiscing with old friends, he was still facing the unknown. He hadn't kept up with any of his company members—a possibility sparking more than a little uncertainty.

Well—it's a wonderful thing when old friends get together, and Bill's reunion was no different. Taking over, they helped him into his Annapolis hotel room, his freshman roommate perhaps his biggest surprise. At that time, Bill could still talk and interact, as well as exhibit facial expressions and, although he was in a wheelchair, he had a fabulous time! Dale enjoyed seeing the animation on his face, knowing he was totally excited about the experience.

There's a lot to be said for normalcy, even if it were only for a second, or two.

After they returned home, Dale kept up with Bill's mates at the Naval Academy, letting them know how things were going— that he was having a hard time.

During that time, Dale had to get used to living on her own. At sixty-seven years old and after forty-six years of marriage, it wasn't an easy transition, so she continued her work where she could give back to anyone who needed her help. Living in the present was something she heard about, but, when it came time for her to make the transition, it wasn't easy. On one occasion, Bill fell, winding up in the hospital—an increasing reminder his disease had a mind of its own, never allowing one to gain control.

It was like living life with a question mark.

"I see him nearly every day," Dale told her daughter when she called to see how her dad was doing. "This week, though, there was a virus going around, so I think it was best I stayed away for a couple of days . . ."

"I know this is tough on you . . ."

Dale was silent for a moment, thinking of her husband. "He's declining," she said, her voice catching on words she never wanted to hear, or say. " I was there for a meeting, and I watched him . . ."

"What do you mean?"

"He was in the background for three hours, and I couldn't help watching him—it brought me to tears . . ." Again, her voice faltered. "When I'm with him, one-on-one, we engage. But, I was seeing your dad as he is during the day—as much as I hate to admit it? It was more than I could take . . ."

"Mom . . ."

"No—you need to know." She paused, gathered herself, then continued. "I had to go in a room to cry, and compose myself. I kind of felt the same way this evening when I saw him . . ."

And, that was the thing—the emotion of dementia never gets easier. Of course, simply due to her work, Dale understood it perfectly. Intellectually. As a family member, however, it was difficult to see it in black and white—understanding was cloaked in shades of grey, as it must have been for their children.

Then, the unthinkable.

"But, much of this is your fault," her daughter screamed with contempt Dale hadn't heard before.

"My fault! How could I have anything to do with it?"

It was then the dam broke, spilling emotions, baring them for all to see. "Because you didn't place him when you should have!"

"But . . ."

Connection severed.

Months passed. As much as Dale hoped she would repair the relationship with her daughter, it wasn't meant to be. Anger seeped into all facets of their lives, causing their children to disengage with their father. Perhaps they thought he'd never know the difference—or, maybe their refusal to be with him throughout his illness was fueled by anger with their mom. Still, with animosity filtering into emotions, Dale understood—after all, it wasn't easy to know someone they loved was deteriorating to a point where he'd no longer recognize them. No longer kiss them.

No longer know a life he loved.

Even so, Dale refused to take the easy way out by keeping them apprised of his condition. She emailed her children weekly, including pictures, letting them know how their father was doing—some days better than others. It was tough—but, she had to allow them to decide how they were going to handle their father's illness, as well as how much they wanted to be involved. There are those, of course, who may consider their decision to disengage selfish—but, were they? Or, was keeping their distance the only way they could cope with the pain, and raw emotion . . .

It's only for them to know.

The hardest part for Dale—and, she suspected it was the same for her children—was the uncertainty of how long they had left with Bill. It was a lament she heard from other families dealing with Alzheimer's or dementia, but, until she experienced it for herself, it didn't hit home. Not to mention, expressing such sentiment could easily go awry, leaving some to think she felt life would be easier without him—and, that wasn't the case. No—it was much simpler than that. Wondering how long her husband had before his passing was based on nothing but uncertainty.

"When families get the diagnosis," she confided to a friend one fall morning when they met for coffee, "they're in for a shock. They have no idea of what's down the road. They'll have no idea of what the end of life is going to be like . . ."

Her friend was quiet for a moment, trying to put herself in that position. "I can imagine it weighs on you . . ."

Dale nodded. "It does—I need to be putting everything in place, so, when we get to that point, he'll be on palliative care."

"What does that mean?"

"Only that his symptoms are being managed—relief from the symptoms and stress of his illness." Dale sighed, resignation evident. "I want to know—when it comes time for hospice—he has what he needs. He needs to be comfortable . . ."

"Do you feel as if you're grieving now?"

"What an interesting question—I guess I am. It's kind of an anticipatory grief. It comes in waves . . ."

"I'm not sure I know what you mean . . ."

"Well, I can be going through my day just fine and, suddenly, I hear or see something that triggers the thought of death. It's kind of weird . . ."

"When did you notice?"

Dale focused on her friend. "At first, I was in complete denial—we were having a family get-together at Bob Evans, and my mom noticed Bill going out the emergency door . . ."

"Was he trying to leave?"

"No—he was looking for the bathroom. When she told me, I didn't want to hear it, although—because of my job—I knew the symptoms. There were signs . . ."

"Geez . . ."

"It's a difficult thing to realize you need professional help when riding the emotional rollercoaster of Alzheimer's in all of it's varied forms. Bill's dealing with Lewy Body Dementia catapulted us into a world we couldn't imagine—and, I didn't realize I needed help until my mom pointed it out. Don't forget, I was dealing with her illness too, and doing so was, undoubtedly, an extra weight. Bill was fairly young when he lost his mom, so, it was no surprise when my mom slipped into that honored position.

When she died . . . well, it was tough on him."

Finally turning conversation to a more pleasant topic, an hour later Dale's childhood friend left and, once again, Dale was alone to shoulder the weight of her husband's illness. As she thought about Bill, her kids, and her life, thoughts turned to her mother.

Fighting two illnesses at one time was difficult, and Dale often recalled her mother's last days. "I'm so worried about you," her mother commented shortly before she passed. "You're going to go back to your life to face what Bill's dealing with . . ."

Her last words to her daughter.

It's safe to say life changed a few times.

Dale's biggest issue was acceptance—she knew once she could get to that point, she could move on. Unfortunately, that was easier said than done, and she wound up approaching daily life in stages, according to his illness. By doing so, she could cope and, as far as anyone could see, she was getting through it pretty well. The question was how long could she keep it up before she started noticing tiny fractures in her strong façade?

In private times, she wondered about their future if it weren't for Bill's illness. But, thinking such things could do no possible good—so, she spent little time in the past, recalling how, that one day, everything shifted.

She always found it interesting her mother was so insightful—she was constantly aware of how her daughter was feeling. She knew when Dale ended up doing things without her husband, it was only because of Bill's illness. He didn't want to go out, and who could blame him? And, when Dale met her girlfriend for some R & R, there was no question it was exactly what she needed—something just for her.

All the while, however, her mind rarely strayed from her most consuming thought of how she was going to move on with her life—it was something she didn't talk about, or confess. Was she still a person? She didn't want to be defined as a caregiver, but, in many ways, that's what she was, and it was one of those things she couldn't have anticipated.

A loss of self.

Such thoughts, of course, weren't particularly beneficial, and she recalled it was her mom who first asked the delicate question. "Do you need to see someone," she asked on a day Dale's resolve to move forward was in jeopardy.

"Yes . . ." Dale's voice was a soft confession.

Soon after, Dale booked an appointment with a therapist—although not many knew, she changed, Bill's diagnosis sparking a raging anger at anyone in the medical profession.

Medical appointments were always a challenge and, if a nurse or doctor did something she didn't like, Dale flew off the handle, targeting her disappointment and anger toward someone she hoped would understand. Completely unable to control herself, she told them off, not sorry she'd done so.

"You've got to be nice," Bill told her one day as they waited for his doctor. "We need their help . . ."

Fortunately, her therapist's specialty was working with caregivers and, although Dale was hopeful she'd gain a little relief, she wasn't counting on it. But, within the first ten minutes of her session, the therapist nailed her struggle—it turned out her anger was all about control.

Dale felt as if she didn't have any.

She certainly couldn't control her husband's illness, could she? Of course not. But, that didn't stop her from trying—and, it was during those times she had to remind herself there would be rough going. Times when she'd lose control. Times when she'd regain it.

She also had to remember things would be okay.

You see, Dale realized people's reactions are different—hers was anger toward the doctors because they delivered the diagnosis. Was her anger misplaced? Yes. Was it understandable? Yes. But, that was the thing—she finally figured out she wasn't blaming them for his illness.

She just wanted them to be perfect.

The only problem with that was they weren't—and, when imperfection raised its ugly head? You get the picture . . . it were as if something ignited. Although she's not proud of her actions, Dale doesn't hesitate to share her reaction to Bill's illness, whether in private conversation, or in a presentation during which topics are Lewy Body, Alzheimer's, and other forms of dementia.

The truth is many people who are caregivers for a loved one struggle with the possibility of losing control—they believe they've lost control of their lives. "If it's any help for anyone going through such difficult times similar to mine," Dale confided during one of the times she needed her friend. "I encourage them to realize when their whole life flips around, they can gain control. It may not feel like it, and they may not think they can—but, they can do it."

Her friend nodded, waiting for her to continue.

"I also encourage anyone in the same situation to seek professional help. It's not a sign of weakness . . .

It's a sign of courage . . ."

CHAPTER SEVEN

The Gem

As Bill's disease progressed, Dale continued to immerse herself in giving back to those who could use her help. Working through emotional hurdles by herself wasn't the way to go, and she wanted family members of those afflicted by memory disease to know she was in their corner.

"You're going to be angry," she told them, "but, eventually, you'll come to accept your situation. Once you do, you'll realize and understand you can't control the disease—and, you can't let it control you." Her words made sense and, as she continued to experience life without her husband at her side, she learned to live by them.

Then came time to tackle the government.

It seemed logical—because Bill was a military vet—he should be entitled to disability benefits. That, of course, proved trickier than it should have been simply because Dale had to prove Bill's disease was *caused* by military negligence.

After considerable research and contacting those who were supposed to get things accomplished, she learned her husband's military base had a problem with toxic water for years due to a dry cleaner's dumping chemicals that leached into the area's groundwater.

Not good.

Up to three million people could have been impacted, and it's only within the last couple of years the V.A. ruled anyone with Parkinson's Disease who was stationed at Camp Lejeune in North Carolina was eligible for full disability. As a result of her research, Dale learned of a proven connection between cancerous tumors and the water at Camp Lejeune, so it stood to reason her husband's Lewy Body Syndrome could be the result of the same gross negligence. It certainly makes sense and, as of this writing, she's still pursuing it.

One more frustration.

"I know it's been tough—but, if you had advice for anyone going through the same thing as us, what would you tell them?"

Chris watched his mom pull a cup from the kitchen cupboard, then a teabag from the canister on the counter.

"Good heavens! I never really thought about it . . ."

"Well, what do you say to people who are just now finding out?"

Dale poured water into a glass measuring cup, then put it in the microwave. "I'd probably tell them to get to a reputable and qualified neurologist . . ." She pushed two buttons, then turned to her son. "It's important to have an accurate—and, early—diagnosis."

Chris nodded. "I agree. I remember when the first guy said Dad had MCI . . ."

Dale shook her head. "Oh, please! I knew it wasn't mild cognitive impairment—at least that doctor had the smarts to send us to Cleveland."

"Thank God for that . . ." Chris was quiet for a moment. "What else?"

"Advice, you mean?"

"Yeah—both of us know there's a lot more to it."

Dale pulled the hot water from the microwave, filled her cup, then joined her son at the table. "Well—the thing that really helped me was education. If someone has Alzheimer's, then reach out to an Alzheimer's association. If it's Lewy Body? Same thing."

"In other words, build your own support system . . ."

Dale looked at him, knowing their lives would again change, and it was only a matter of time.

"Exactly . . ."

As months pass—sometimes slowly, sometimes as if it can't fly by quickly enough—Dale lives her days with the knowledge at some time in the foreseeable future, her life will change dramatically. Trying not to live within a circle of despair, she keeps busy with her life with Bill, as well as the new life she knows she must build after his passing. There's much to be said for knowing where you're going before you get there—a wisdom sometimes impossible to capture.

Of course, knowing Bill's illness is certainly capable of fracturing relationships simply because of emotion, it's important to remain a tight family unit no matter the challenge. She and her family realized they can't let that happen, so each family member deals with his or her personal moments of grief—knowing what's before them—as best they can.

But . . . it ain't easy.

Newfound wisdom, however, offers Dale the opportunity for understanding on many different levels, and she hopes to pay it forward by supporting those who are traveling—or, have yet to travel—her path.

So, life continues to shift for her, as well as her children—as it does, she's comforted by understanding memories will, eventually, be all she has. But, within those memories is the gem—the little nugget—which will always prompt a smile. Her favorite?

A simple photograph of her children, and Bill.

It wasn't anything special, or planned—the boy's were sitting at Bill's knee looking up at him, his daughter standing behind with her hand on his head. As with many of their family photographs, it was taken shortly after Thanksgiving in 2018, yet Dale didn't realize what she captured until she looked at the snapshot after returning home from a visit. It was then she discovered the sliver of hope and inspiration she desperately needed.

Reconnection.

JUDY HOLSGROVE

CHAPTER EIGHT

Judy

Childhood. To most, it's a time of learning about life. Joy. Happiness. It's when the bond with parents strengthens, creating an impermeable feeling of protection, as well as a time when a child can create or explore with positive encouragement. At least, that's the way it should be—but, as you undoubtedly know, that's not always the way it is. For Judy?

A Catholic orphanage.

One of seven children, her mother decided she could no longer care for all of them. So, Judy and two siblings were shipped off to Staten Island to be raised by nuns, some loving and kind, others harsh and scolding. But, as time passed, she did the best with what she had, finally leaving the second she turned eighteen. Then? Marriage. Three kids. Divorce. About two years shy of a decade ensconced in not-so-marital bliss, Judy decided to call it quits, taking a chance on being a single mom.

And, it worked, too. It turned out she was pretty darned good at caring for her children and, when they finally flew the nest, she could rest easy her job was well done. It wasn't until 2014—while she was still living in New York—things started to change.

"I don't know, Diane—there's something about Mom that isn't quite right . . ." Donna sighed, uncertain if her sister noticed.

"What do you mean?"

"Well, the main thing is she's starting to be . . . forgetful. I tell her something, and she doesn't retain it—know what I mean?"

"Honestly, I haven't noticed—but, you see her all the time, and I only talk to her on the phone. It makes sense you're going to notice the changes." Diane paused. "Do you think it's serious?"

"I don't know—maybe it's aging." Another pause. "I just don't know. All I can tell you is something isn't right . . ."

"Have you taken her to the doctor?"

"Not yet . . ."

Diane hesitated, knowing her sister had her hands full. "Maybe it's time . . ."

Silence.

"Donna—what if it's Alzheimer's? Or, something like it? You and I know Mom isn't forgetful!"

"I know. I think that's what I'm afraid of . . ."

"Have you talked to Billy?"

"Not yet . . ."

"Do you think," Diane asked, her voice slightly strained, "it has anything to do with Dad's dying?"

"I don't know—it's been two years, so I kind of doubt it."

Their mother's memory issue was a concern for both daughters, and it was a realization neither wanted to admit—or, ignore. It was clear her life—and, their's—was changing.

The question was what to do . . .

As you can imagine, initial conversations consisted of the best living situation for their mother. Diane lived in Colorado, Donna in New York . . . and, Billy? Well, it didn't really matter—he wasn't involved in the decision, and it was better he learned of plans through one of his sisters.

"She can live with me," Diane advised during one of their many conversations after Judy's official diagnosis.

"But—you don't have any idea of what it's like. Are you sure?"

"How can I know what it's like being around her? All I have to judge this entire situation is by phone conversations—it's a completely different dynamic!"

Donna was quiet, thinking of how her life was about to change. She lived close to her mother for years, and it was nothing to bop over to say hi, or have a cup of coffee and a cigarette together before both of them quit. "It's going to be weird—first dad, now Mom."

In that moment, Diane understood. "I know—your life will be different without her so close. But, we have to look at the logical perspective—and, I think living with me is the best way to go. And, you were the one taking care of Dad when I couldn't be there because I live across the country. I think it's my turn . . ." For a brief moment she thought of Billy, quickly discounting the possibility of much help from him. "I want to do it . . ."

And, that was it. Decision made. No sales pitch.

Judy was on her way to Colorado.

The physical move was—as moves go—fairly easy. Judy agreed, and Donna was responsible for packing her mom's belongings, as well as making sure she had creature comforts providing what some might consider the smallest pleasure. But, as Judy's illness escalated, it was the small things she needed in her life.

During the moving process, Diane was painfully aware how difficult Judy's relocating was on her sister. Their dad's passing was trying enough, and Diane often wondered if her sister truly recovered from her grief—although Donna said otherwise, Diane wasn't so sure. But, in truth, when their dad died, it was hard on Diane, too—it was a loss both daughters felt. So, to take Judy away from her daughter? A bitter pill . . .

One consideration Diane thought important was the differences in their lives—Diane adopted a son when she was forty, and her sister's children were older, placing them at different phases of life. It was that fact tipping the moving scale toward Colorado—she was already in the mode of caring for someone.

So, Judy moved in with Diane, and things were going smoothly—until Judy decided she didn't want to live with her daughter, anymore. The idea of living with a young child was less than appealing, and she despised the noise—a reaction her two daughters didn't anticipate, both surmising it had a lot to do with her growing up in the orphanage. Even so, there was always an element of the 'grass is always greener' to their mom's personality. It was the 'next place will be better' thing, and, such a mindset proved a trying battle. For whatever reason, it was impossible for Judy to be satisfied with what she had, or with the here and now.

It was that dissatisfaction spawning moves to different rooms within Diane's home, until there were no more rooms as an option. "Maybe I'm enabling her," Diane confessed to her sister during their weekly catch-up call. "But, I want her to be happy . . ."

"I get it—but, you moved her three times within your house! Do you really think you can handle her living with you?"

"Yes!" A pause. "Maybe . . ."

"That's what I thought . . ." Donna was quiet, knowing her sister was conflicted. "Maybe—maybe it's time we look at assisted living . . ."

"Really? Do you think it's coming to that?"

"Yes! You see the decline—the fact is it's not going to get any better."

Tough words to hear.

Tough to admit.

When Diane broached the subject with Judy, she was all for it—such a move would provide the independence she craved.

Maybe.

While living with her daughter, Judy's decline was no surprise and, when Diane arrived home to the smell of acrid smoke, she rushed into her mom's room, spying a t-shirt on an electric heater. In that moment, she knew—the barren realization her mother's safety was in peril, as was Diane's and her son's. But, even with that knowledge, there was no decision to move her to a facility with round-the-clock care.

That didn't come until Judy accused Diane's son of stealing money—yet, it would always show up. Clearly, he didn't steal anything. "He has whatever he wants," Diane confided to Donna. "He doesn't need to steal . . ."

"I know—I'm pretty sure she forgot where she put it."

Another stark truth, prompting a stark conversation with Judy a few days later. "Mom—do you want to be here?"

"No."

Although her mother's words stung, Diane knew it was how her mom truly felt. "Well, then—maybe it's time we look for something else."

Enter assisted living.

Remember the grass is always greener thing? Well, that's the way it was when Diane moved Judy into a studio apartment at an assisted living facility—until that didn't work, and she insisted on a one bedroom because she wanted more of her stuff. Certainly understandable, but it was difficult on Diane having to move her every few months, back and forth. Back and forth.

Back and forth.

Soon, it was clear Judy needed full-time care. Similar to the incident with the electric heater, Diane walked into her mom's room to discover her mom sitting in a wheelchair, soiled. "No one's here to help me," Judy cried, tears streaming onto her cheeks.

Understandably, Diane was incensed. *How is this possible,* she screamed silently. Then, she screamed the same words to anyone who was listening.

Naturally, apologies were served—all with the underlying excuse Judy needed full-time care. "She's beyond our capabilities here," the administrative coordinator told her.

"Are you sure?"

"Yes—she needs care at the next level."

"What does that mean?"

"Memory care . . ."

Another move.

Having gained a bit of knowledge about Alzheimer's, there were a few things Diane considered imperative when deciding on the right facility for her mom—it had to be close to her, and provide a homey atmosphere not resembling a huge hotel. With that in mind, as soon as she found Applewood Our House, she knew it was the right place. *She'll be happy here*, she thought as she met with Applewood's intake coordinator.

Another decision made.

But, there was just one, little glitch—the facility was in the process of being constructed. There were art and design renderings of the facility's rooms, and three were already taken—so, of the rooms remaining, she chose the one with the most sunlight, and was excited about the thought of moving in.

A decision Judy immediately regretted, possibly due to the Grass is Always Greener Syndrome.

"Mom—you chose the room you wanted! Not only that, we paid the deposit!"

It was an argument she wasn't sure her mother understood.

Visits were emotionally charged and, unfortunately, things didn't get any better as time inched by. Every time Diane visited, her mother cried, making it nearly impossible for her daughter to leave—and, when she did, Judy cried, too. The situation provided a rock-and-a-hard place moment, and it was clear whatever Diane did or didn't do, it was never enough. The truth was she could have visited every day, and the tears wouldn't have changed.

Then? Rules.

A constant source of irritation, Diane understood their necessity, but Judy didn't care for living under someone's watchful eye—especially when it came to her wine. Of course, Judy and Diane were of the opinion one glass an evening was fine—what could it hurt? The assisted living big guns, however, saw it differently, and it wasn't until after a few emotional conversations did they relent.

After that, it was clear Judy's first assisted living facility higher-ups wanted her gone.

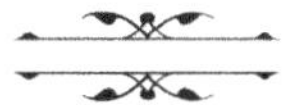

Weeks passed.

Judy was constantly upset, and Diane—well, she was trying to keep it together. It wasn't until Applewood Our House opened its facility did things begin to get better, and Diane began to feel a sense of relief knowing her mom was in a safe place. She had a trip planned for a long time and, until Judy moved to Applewood, she wasn't sure she should go. But, the truth was she needed a break—a bit of time to enjoy herself without thinking of all the things she had to do next.

With only a few days before her departure, it was clear the atmosphere at Applewood was loving, and kind. Rules were always in force, of course, but they weren't as stringent as Judy's previous facility. The only thing really bothering her was she wasn't allowed to have her own toothpaste—a safety concern regarding other residents.

When Diane explained it to her, Judy didn't much care for that answer—she wanted to brush her teeth whenever she wanted with her own toothpaste. But, it's important to remember, at that time, Judy's Alzheimer's progression wasn't rapid—much of her life was relatively normal, and it was tough adjusting to the progression of her illness.

The first six months at Applewood were trying, and Diane didn't know what mood her mother would be in when she walked in the door. Sometimes, she'd be smiling and, other times, she would be the target of Judy's complaints and accusations. Often, it seemed as if Judy were equating Diane with her mother who abandoned her, sending her off to the orphanage—and, when Diane thought about it, there was a modicum of the abandonment issue making sense. Still, Diane suspected there was another reason for her mom's somewhat incorrigible behavior . . .

Being shuttled off to a facility wasn't part of the plan.

Initially, as you may recall, Judy was to live with Diane until the progression of her disease worsened—an arrangement initially thought best for Judy, and Diane. Plus, Judy had a finite amount of money, and living with Diane would be more cost-effective. But, as you know, things change, and Judy wasn't quite ready to succumb to the limitations of her illness.

It was, perhaps, the most important factor making the transition difficult.

It wasn't until her sister visited six months after Judy moved into Applewood Our House did Diane feel a sense of relief. "I know it's tough," Donna commented after visiting her mom, "but, she's in the right place. You did the right thing . . ."

"She's always telling me she wants to move . . ."

"I know—but, it's clear you can't allow that to happen. She's past the point of living with you or me, and she needs the full-time care . . ."

"Have you talked Billy?"

"A little . . ."

Both women were silent as fleeting memories took them back to a time when things were different. "Well, that's his decision—we have to move forward, and do the best thing possible for Mom," Donna confirmed. "And, that's exactly what we'll do . . ."

"I agree—but, I'm a little worried about it."

"She always loved Christmas . . ."

"I know—I want to recreate a Christmas that will be familiar to her, but I'm not sure she'll understand." A pause. "But, that's not the hardest part—her understanding, I mean."

"I'm not sure I know what you mean . . ."

Diane focused on her sister. "It's the conversations—we used to have meaningful conversations, and now we just talk about how we're going to save the world."

Donna was quiet, understanding how her sister felt. "I know it's tough on you—and, I'm sorry. I can see how her slipping away from our familiar lives hurts you . . ."

"I really think it's the hardest part . . ." Diane's voice caught, knowing life would never be the same.

CHAPTER NINE

Pulling up Socks

When challenging illness strikes, it often eclipses everything, including wonderful memories of the past—at least, that's how it seems. No longer did Judy recall Christmas's when the kids were young, or their holiday plans which were always the same.

Even though Judy and her husband divorced, they did everything to make the holidays a time of joy for their children—something they appreciated as they got older. Christmas Eve was always with Dad, and they spent Christmas Day with Judy—it was a tradition that worked well, and seldom were there feelings of being uncomfortable because their parents were no longer together. Judy and her ex-husband were solid on making things as normal as possible and, when the kids were young, their dad would drop off presents long after their bedtime, as if Santa visited during their excited slumber.

It was all about the magic . . .

Those were the good times, Diane thought as she sipped a cup of hot chocolate, enjoying the Christmas tree with her son—and, in that moment, it were as if she were sitting at the kitchen table with her mom and sister in New York, Judy and Donna smoking cigarettes, and chatting—you know, the kind of conversation kids have with their parents after they fly the nest. It's a different kind of communication—parenting is over, and each can enjoy the other on a different level.

Memories continued to flow, Diane clearly recalling when Judy moved to live with her, they'd sit on Diane's deck sipping wine, Judy wearing the hat she refused to give up. In fact, her hat was so much a part of her, each daughter had dibs—so, one day, Diane took a pic, and sent it to her sister so she could have a little piece of her mother.

"I cried when I got it," Donna confessed.

"It's the only thing I want, you know . . ."

"I know—I want it, too."

It was too bad when shortly after their conversation, the hat wound up in the washer and dryer accidentally—and, that was the end of it. Little did Diane know when she saw a recent photo and sent it to her sister, it would become a fond memory of the past.

One neither would forget.

So, as Judy's memory continues to fade, there's more water to flow under the bridge—such a journey is never easy, its ups and downs fleeting and frequent. Alzheimer's was difficult for both daughters, and Judy often commented on the need for patience. "It's hard" Diane told her sister on the phone recently.

"I know—although, it has to be more difficult for you because you're living it every day." Donna paused. "If you had the opportunity to sit down with someone who's walking the same path, what advice would you give them?"

"Seriously?"

"Yes—seriously. You've learned a lot, and I think it's important."

"Well—you already know I think patience is key. And . . . it's no one's fault."

"What do you mean?"

"You know mom struggles with independence she wants it still, to some degree, and she can't have it. I can't imagine what that feels like—I sometimes wonder if she blames herself, or one of us for her situation. When she gets like that, I have to be patient . . ."

"I know exactly what you mean . . ."

Diane was quiet, thinking of her mom. "It's like she's not very kind to herself . . ."

"I can't imagine . . ."

Again, both were quiet, until Donna broke the emotional silence. "What's the most important thing you learned from Mom?

Diane laughed. "I don't have to think about that one—independence! She was one independent woman—having the guts to get out of her marriage, and raise three kids on her own was something I'm not sure I could have done!"

"I know. She taught me to go after what I wanted in life—nobody could hold me back if I had the courage!" Donna paused. "When I think about her living in an orphanage . . . well, she didn't have any role models and, as you know, the family dynamic was important to her . . ."

"Yep—she always believes in family. And, we're to be there for each other, no matter what . . ."

Donna sniffled, trying to stifle the tears she knew were coming. "Sometimes, I think of the other kids at the orphanage—you know, what their lives turned out to be. When I think of them, I can't help but think how lucky we are to have a mom who had the guts to get out as soon as she could . . ."

"Do you think living in the orphanage damaged her in any way?"

Donna thought about her sister's question before answering. "I don't think so—I prefer to believe it taught her about survival, and the things she needed to know about life before striking out on her own."

"But, what about . . ."

"The truth is it really doesn't matter. She never showed us signs of her younger years causing her a bunch of grief—in fact, it was the other way around."

"You're right—all we can do now is make her life as comfortable and happy as possible. She's a strong woman, and I hope we can carry on that legacy . . ."

And, that's where they left it—Diane knowing her mom is in the best place possible, also knowing coming months will be fraught with challenges. It's in those times of realization she knows she must be strong—not only her, but her sister and brother, as well. The time will come when they must draw on everything their mother taught them—to pull up their socks when the going gets tough, and lean on her strength for she will always be with them. With her at their side, they'll have courage, and the power to do . . .

Anything.

SHIRLEY ENWALL

CHAPTER TEN

SHIRLEY

*S*hirley Enwall was a western gal. Eclectic. A little bit different. Most of her life she lived in Denver, only a few times leaving the comfort of her Rocky Mountain home as she was growing up. As an adult?

Denver was it from the time she was nineteen years old.

Creative and exceptionally social, she loved the easy-going lifestyle for which the West was so well-known and, when she met the man of her dreams?

Everything was perfect.

She and Roger Enwall married and, as you might guess, little ones weren't far behind—which was great because grandparents lived down the street. It couldn't have been a better set-up, and it's where the happy family lived for years. Then, a few different homes, but they were always careful to stay in the Denver area—and, why wouldn't they?

Living at the base of the Rocky Mountains filled Shirley's soul.

But, there was nothing she and her husband loved more than Eastern Star, and the Masons. He was also involved with the Elks organization, achieving 'grand poobah' status in both, maintaining his standings for years. Shirley? She, too, achieved poobah status, and loved dressing up—you know, long white gloves, and the whole bit.

Shirley's unique personality was evident from the time she was a child—loving, and full of life. Unfortunately, however, it was also a time of illness—rheumatic fever three times, and it's a strong probability the neurotransmitters in her brain were damaged. It's also a strong possibility the fever caused her Alzheimer's so many years later . . .

But, for some reason, her dementia was different—not the regular, familial Alzheimer's, and it's accompanying stages. Shirley bounced all over the place, her behavior different than others fighting the disease—but, as they grew older, her children, Leah Ann, Scott, and Vicky noticed the little things.

"I don't know how to describe it," Leah Ann mentioned to her brother one day. "She seems . . . distant."

"She also asks a lot of questions because she doesn't remember stuff . . ."

"I know—and, it frustrates Dad. In fact, I think it goes a little further than that . . . he talked to me about it, and I had to tell him it's just Mom."

Scott was quiet. "Maybe she should have it checked out . . ."

"That's what I told him . . ."

And, that's exactly what Shirley did—a neurologist examined her, conducting tests, finally diagnosing her with Alzheimer's, although the doc didn't call it that—more dementia, he said. But, that was about eighteen years ago, and her diagnosis wasn't the most accurate. Unfortunately, it came long before discovering the different stages and types of Alzheimer's.

Doctors suggested Shirley try one of the newest drugs on the market, but Roger had serious reservations—it was still in trial periods. "What are the side effects," her husband asked during one of their consultations.

"Well—if Shirley begins taking it, she can never go off of it. It will kill her . . ."

Bombshell.

Clearly, Shirley and Roger had a decision to make. Roger grappled with the knowledge he had to do the best thing for his wife, so he discussed the situation with Leah Ann, finally deciding to go ahead with the medication.

It's just how it needed to be.

One issue he had to deal with immediately was his wife's behavior. She was forgetting this and that, also developing an itch to spend money.

A lot of it.

Still, Roger didn't say a word—it was just . . . Mom.

Then, 2014.

Big changes.

Roger passed away, leaving Leah Ann to manage Shirley's daily life, including funds. It was something his daughter didn't realize was so—difficult. Keeping track was a formidable task and, on top of that, she knew her mom needed another clinical evaluation. Up until that point, no one officially diagnosed Shirley with Alzheimer's.

It was time.

So, Leah Ann made an appointment with the neurologist soon after Roger's passing—he passed in December, and they were lucky to get an appointment in January. "Will you explain to Mom and me her exact diagnosis," Leah Ann requested. "And, how should we move forward . . ."

"Well, her diagnosis has always been Alzheimer's . . ."

Another bombshell.

"That's the first time we've heard that . . ."

For Shirley, as well, the official diagnosis was tough to accept. "I don't have Alzheimer's," she would say repeatedly, her denial obvious to family members and friends.

But, Shirley never remembered the denial.

Since that tough, life-altering conversation, Shirley's condition deteriorated, albeit slowly. She stayed on her first-prescribed medication for quite awhile, and it wasn't until recently there was a need to change. Her slow decline wasn't typical, and it was difficult to determine exactly where she was emotionally—they were changing significantly.

As time passed, Leah Ann and her siblings noticed Alzheimer's doesn't allow for any kind of emotional level—in fact, when Leah Ann's and Scott's sister, Vicky, passed ten years ago, Leah Ann never saw her mom cry. Of course, she might have, but it's reasonable to think family members would have noticed. Occasionally, she refers to Vicky, but never accompanied by tears. It was the same when her husband passed—the only time she cried was when the kids brought his ashes back to their home. Even then, it wasn't what they expected—all she said was, "Oh, my God."

That was it.

It were as if the emotional part of her brain shut down. No tears for her mother's passing, her sister's, or her little dog's. Nothing. The whole experience was odd, especially since Shirley was the one who cried at television shows, and commercials.

Throughout it all, her disconnect continued to widen.

"We still have a connection," Leah Ann confirmed to her brother. "But, it's . . . distant." She wasn't sure he'd understand—he wasn't around much, trusting his sister to make the right decisions.

He did. "I know—if we go to hug or kiss her, she recoils."

"It's weird, too—ever since I can remember, Mom was the one we went to for hugs and smooches. You know . . . for love."

"I wonder if that bothered Dad," Scott asked, recalling his father's more staid personality.

"I have no idea—I never asked, and he didn't say."

Both were quiet for a moment, thinking about the past, as well as the future. "Do you remember when we first suspected," Leah Ann asked. "It seems so long ago . . ."

"Some of it—I think my first memories are from when Dad talked about it. In fact, he was the one who noticed she was different . . ."

"It was when she started forgetting things . . ."

"Mom must have been in her early eighties—but, honestly, I don't really remember."

"I think that's right—and, he thought he would be there forever to take care of her."

"Then, he dropped dead from a heart attack . . ."

Leah Ann was silent, thinking of her mom and dad. "You just never know . . ."

Leah Ann began looking for the right facility for her and, as you can imagine, once that process began, there was a stream of never-ending information. It wasn't until after reviewing what they had to offer did she discover Applewood Our House.

Transition is always difficult—leaving familiarity for something unknown is scary. So, when Leah Ann decided to move Shirley from her family home to Applewood, there was no question quality of life would be better. Recently, Leah Ann made the decision to take Shirley off the medication slated to kill her—she figured eighteen years was long enough, and it was time to let the illness progress, not prolonging her life. Knowing the importance of a quality life, they wanted the best for their mom.

After Shirley's husband passed, she was by herself for a while—yes, family and friends kept her on their radar, always there to keep watch, protecting Shirley as best they could, but she was still spending money at an alarming rate. Leah Ann finally had to take her to the bank, so Shirley could add her to her accounts. If she hadn't insisted?

Shirley would have wound up in the poor farm sooner, than later.

They knew, however, the transition from home to Applewood wasn't going to be easy. So, she went for a first visit, meeting with the intake coordinator. After in-depth conversation, both decided Applewood was a good fit for Shirley, and they moved forward with transitioning. The fact Leah Ann had power of attorney for her mom made things easier, but, just to make sure things progressed smoothly, she became her legal guardian, as well.

Even so, transitioning Shirley from her home to Applewood was a long, arduous process. She, of course, was in a constant state of denial, and Leah Ann found herself having to be the bad guy. "I'm in charge now," she told her, naming off things needing to be accomplished. "This is what we're going to do . . ." Otherwise, she wouldn't have gone and, when they talked about it, Shirley wasn't one hundred percent on board with Applewood.

"What we're going to do," Leah Ann finally instructed, "is pack a suitcase—like you're going on vacation. Then, there will be a day I'll come over—and, I won't tell you when. But, that will be your move-out day . . ." It was the only way it could work because, otherwise, Shirley would fixate on a day and time.

And, that's exactly how transitioning Shirley went down. With people to help, they marked all of her clothes, going through her stuff, making sure she had what she needed for a couple of weeks. Her dog went to Leah Ann's house, living there until she passed.

Then, it was time. With a friend, Leah Ann took Shirley to Applewood Our House—her room was already set up with familiar furniture her mom picked out including a small table, and her favorite chair. But, perhaps the most important thing? Shirley helped put her clothes away, filling the closet with what needed to be on hangars.

Such small actions helped with the transition, but the truth was Shirley was still anxious. After the first six weeks at Applewood? Her thoughts were filled with only one thing.

Escape.

And, she did.

One thing Leah Ann didn't consider when transitioning her mom was Shirley's ability to become Houdini, and a mini-MacGyver—she could use anything to fix, break, or destroy things. So, what did Shirley do?

Climbed out the window, and split.

Fortunately, a mile-and-a-half from Applewood Our House, the police found her. Unfortunately, it wasn't the first and only time—her escape-artist talent was legend and, on one of her treks, she happened upon a woman working in her yard. "I don't know how to get to my home," Shirley told her, and it was then the woman noticed Shirley held a grocery bag with a bottle of water, boxed candy, a pair of shoes, and a pair of pants. Nothing else. No coat, no nothin'.

Well, the woman knew instantly something was off, so she convinced Shirley to go the police station, then helped her to get in the car.

It was the right thing to do, but all Shirley could remember was her old address, and that's where the policeman took her. It was only by the grace of good luck a neighbor recognized Shirley, telling the policeman about Shirley's move to a facility somewhere. Since Applewood called to report her missing, he put two and two together.

In the meantime, the search began, and Applewood contacted Leah Ann in Longmont, a town north of Denver. By the time she got to Shirley's former address, Shirley was getting ready for a trip to the hospital—just to make sure everything checked out.

They did, and it was back to Applewood. Shortly after the incident, they changed Shirley's medication, taking her off those causing anxiety, and she's been fine since then.

Her last escape was her greatest escape.

So, how did she do it? The first time, they caught her trying to go over the fence. She removed the gate, neatly placing the parts beside the fencepost—then in a dim garden, she lifted off the gate, and she was gone.

Only to be apprehended a few blocks away.

Other times, they caught her trying to follow people out the back door—very cagey. Unfortunately for Shirley, however, Applewood upped its security, and their Houdini was reined in.

She finally adjusted, calling Applewood home, and that's where she became comfortable. If Leah Ann and her husband picked Shirley up for a holiday get-together, it wasn't long before she wanted to go home—that's why they don't do much on the weekends, anymore.

Shirley simply wanted to go home to Applewood Our House.

Having her in a safe environment was infinitely better than Shirley's being in her own home—when they tried that, Leah Ann's daughter, Shirley's granddaughter, moved in with her, but it turned out to be a toxic situation. Shirley couldn't remember, but she said hurtful things—something she would never do if it weren't for her illness, although, as the disease progressed, she was sharp-tongued.

It was clear life continued to shift for Leah Ann, and her family. What they knew and loved was slipping from their fingers, and there wasn't a thing they could do about it.

Not a darned thing . . .

CHAPTER ELEVEN

Life Unexpected

For some reason, we often choose to keep things to ourselves during stressful times, not wanting to burden others with our problems—and, it seems that's what was going through Roger's mind when Shirley's symptoms manifested. Leah Ann felt more than once she wished her dad would have said something sooner—why he didn't, she isn't exactly sure, but, it's a good bet he didn't want her to worry.

That's what parents do, isn't it?

But, Leah Ann did worry. Anxiety reared its ugly head when planning Shirley's move—was it best for her mom? How would she react moving to an unfamiliar place? All questions she would have loved to have answered, but the fact was until

Leah Ann went through the process, there would be no answers to her internal questions. She figured family members of other Alzheimer's patients probably felt the same way, but knowing that didn't ease the emotional pain. The move was critical, and she was the one to do it.

A lot for anyone's plate.

Thinking things through, she couldn't help but think of her father, recalling how difficult his wife's decline was on him. If he told Leah Ann at the onset of Shirley's illness, maybe things wouldn't have been so tough on him—maybe he wouldn't have struggled so much.

Recalling how life was before Applewood, Leah Ann was well aware Shirley's behavior was no picnic—a stubborn woman, she always needed to do things her way. When it came time to tell her she could no longer drive, the conversation wasn't pretty. Most days, it was a battle royale. "Mom," Leah Ann told her, "we took the car away. You're hitting people . . ."

Of course, Shirley was defiant, refusing to believe any such thing. "I'm not hitting them—they're hitting me!"

There was no question Shirley's recollection of such events wasn't accurate. There were days her mom would take the car, only to return with dings obviously caused by her plowing into something—not the other way around.

And, so it went.

Shirley's freedom slowly waned, leaving Leah Ann to wonder what it must be like to lose self-reliance. Hindsight did no good, so all she could do was move forward, trying to be the best daughter possible. It was tough, though, to learn her mom was pilfering liquor and eggnog from the neighborhood store. No one would have known had Leah Ann's daughter, Lindsay, not ratted her out.

"Mom—there's a quart of eggnog that has Southern Comfort in it in the refrigerator . . ."

"What?"

"I'm not kidding! I saw it when I got home from work!"

Well, that was completely unacceptable. When Lindsay agreed to live with her grandmother before her move to Applewood, she didn't anticipate such issues. But, how could she? Shirley's Alzheimer's was new for everyone, and there wasn't a rule book on what to expect, do, or say.

So, at her mother's request, Lindsay piled Shirley in the car, returning to the liquor store. "Was this woman in here today," she asked the man standing behind the counter as she and Shirley crossed the threshold.

"Well . . . yes."

She plopped the items Shirley stole in front of him. "Do not do business with this woman under any circumstances—she has no money, and she stole this stuff today. If she comes in, watch her—and, please call my mom, or someone . . ."

Slightly stunned, the proprietor agreed. Lindsay gave him contact numbers for her mom and her, and he was pretty good about it because they didn't press charges. The whole episode, however, was kind of a mess, and it served to school Shirley's family about Alzheimer's. The main thing?

It was the end of Shirley's freedom.

Her propensity for sticky fingers didn't diminish once she moved into Applewood Our House. She'd sneak into residents' rooms, steal what she wanted, then retreat to her own room. But, if those who were victims of her klepto tendencies approached her room?

She pitched a snarky fit.

As Leah Ann saw it, fair was fair. Not so with Shirley—she considered the stolen items hers, and returning them wasn't within the realm of possibility. Not only that, if someone did retrieve what she stole, Shirley considered it stealing from her.

Sadly, it wasn't only residents of Applewood who were feeling the result of Shirley's talent. At Christmas, Leah Ann had to put a baby gate across the stairs because her mom would sneak down, lift what she wanted, then hide it in her purse. Nothing big, but just weird, little stuff.

Those had to be sad moments for her family—they knew Shirley wouldn't steal from anyone in a million years! At least, she didn't used to . . .

Shirley's illness prompted questions about her changing behavior—was her kleptomania coming to the fore because of the progression of the Alzheimer's?

No one was sure.

All the while, Shirley's personality was changing. Before Alzheimer's, she loved living life with abandon, perhaps one reason she loved the West. Life was relaxed, and she made the most of it, filling her days with laughter, and fun. But, as Alzheimer's tightened its grip, she started to morph into someone

Leah Ann's family barely knew—reticent. Fearful. Afraid of making a mistake. Whatever might be happening at Applewood, she refused to take part, embarrassed by the thought she might do something incorrectly.

When Shirley started working with Lisa, the Montessori gal, she said Shirley refused to complete any projects. "I see a step back and, in your mom's mind, she's making some sort of mistake," Lisa informed Leah Ann, "even though there are no mistakes to be made."

Shirley's life was changing in ways no one anticipated—some days good, some bad. Whatever she chose to tackle, whether it were stealing or running away, she did it with zeal. "At least," Leah Ann told her brother, "she has the wherewithal to ask someone if she gets in trouble . . ."

"Seriously? From what you told me, I don't know . . ."

"What scares me is what can happen to her—at least, that one time she ran away, the cops had her. What happens if she runs into someone who'll take advantage of her? What if she falls? Or, gets run over by a car . . ."

"I know—I get it."

"You know what's worse?" Leah Ann didn't wait for his answer. "I can't get into her mind, at all, to figure out what's going on . . ."

"And?" Scott didn't take his eyes from hers.

"Then I get mad—but, when I back away, I realize she doesn't have any idea of what she's doing. I feel guilty . . ."

"You're right," any one can take advantage of her . . ."

"Remember when the cops took her to the old house, and they saw the neighbor?"

"Yeah . . ."

"Well, she never went to the old house, at all . . ."

"Where did she go?"

"The neighbor's . . ."

"What's so bad about that?"

Leah Ann was quiet, recounting the scene in her mind. "Because her supposed—neighbor—was a pretty big influence on Mom."

"In what way?"

"After Dad died? She took Mom to the bank, and had her name put on Mom's accounts . . . and, before we corralled Mom's spending, she'd go to the grocery store with her, wrack up a four hundred dollar bill, and Mom would come home with one little grocery bag."

"Did you ask her about it?"

"Of course, I did! I asked her where the rest of the groceries were, and she said she didn't know. When I found out the neighbor was involved, I hit the ceiling!"

Scott said he understood, but, after hanging up, Leah Ann wondered if her brother had any idea of what was happening with their mother. She kept him apprised of course, but, hearing about it isn't the same as being embroiled in the day to day. When Shirley returned to Applewood the day of her great escape, she didn't understand why she couldn't go see her neighborhood friend, even though Leah Ann tried to make it clear she wasn't a positive influence in her life. Shirley thought the neighbor was the be all and end all when it came to being a friend, so it didn't sit well with her when Leah Ann put the kibosh on her visiting.

Permanently.

As Leah Ann saw it, being Shirley's legal guardian came in handy.

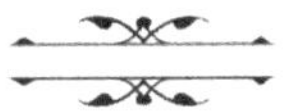

As time passed, it became more difficult to recall the wonderful days after Shirley's diagnosis. When asked to recount the best day with her mom, doing so became more difficult to pinpoint—still, Leah Ann tells of times when, shortly after the diagnosis, her dad and mom laughed together at the silliest things. There was no question they were happy together, their antics akin to a comedy team. Roger had his hands full with Shirley, but he had a sense of humor about it, too—and, when the situation called for it, he'd try to be stern, but it never worked.

Then, sometimes, there's good fortune difficult to explain. As things turned out after Shirley's becoming a resident of Applewood Our House, Leah Ann was offered and accepted a position there, allowing her the opportunity to spend more time with her mom. Never did she think her life would take such a path, but, she feels Applewood is where she needs to be.

As someone who's often asked about what advice she'd give someone beginning the Alzheimer's journey, she always talks of the denial. "The denial has to go away," she tells family members. "I understand it, but it will do no good, and there's nothing they can do to change it."

And, that's the thing about Alzheimer's and, dementia. There's nothing anyone can do, but treat the symptoms. It's not going away, and it's not going to get better—so, it doesn't help to be what she calls the 'helicopter daughter.' "I have to do this . . ." or, "I have to do that . . ." Constantly.

Finally, after witnessing Leah Ann's personal torment of not knowing what to do, an Applewood caregiver advised her with comforting words. "Let us take care of your mom—all you have to do is be her daughter."

Weight lifted.

That's another thing Leah Ann wishes all family members of Alzheimer's patients would understand—the anxiety. There's so much denial coupled with the question . . .

How can we take care of her?

Of course, family members want the best for the person struggling with the disease, but they'll always wonder if they're doing the right thing. But, here's the thing—second guessing will never get anything accomplished. So, how do you know what you're doing is right? The best thing? The thing making you feel better? Well, Leah Ann discovered it comes down to one thing . . .

Faith.

Families have to take the leap of faith, and go forward—living life in the rearview mirror does no one any good. But, as you might imagine, such a leap is difficult—it must be done by trusting the staff and managers to give the best of themselves when caring for their residents.

It's not easy placing a loved one in caring hands other than your own—doing so depends on faith. Trust. The ability to let go. When family members achieve those three things—faith, trust, and the ability to let go—something interesting happens. Things you thought impossible, difficult, or unpleasant take on a different sheen—one of clarity, and knowledge. When that happens—according to family members of Alzheimer's patients—the weight lifts, and the burden of knowing what life holds for their loved one becomes lighter. Why? It's really pretty simple—Alzheimer's and dementia run their own game.

You have no control.

All you can control is how you deal with it.

Even though it's a game that can't be won, family members can choose the way they want to play—and, it empowers them to deal with the often unplanned and serendipitous daily difficulties they may encounter. Although life may prove unbearable in the early stages of the disease, one thing remains constant in the lives of Alzheimer's family members—calm eventually fills them when stark realization is replaced with love, and acceptance.

When you first notice your family member can't find their keys, you probably don't think much about it—Leah Ann didn't when Shirley's behavior began to change slightly. The fact is Alzheimer's or dementia was somewhere in the recesses of her mind, and she chalked up her mom's slight forgetfulness to age— not a permanently failing memory. But, when those tiny changes shape shifted into something more—well, you know the story.

As time inches by, you'll learn how to respond. React. Reply. There will be times frustration mounts to the point where you think you just can't deal with it, anymore.

But, you can.

Heartbreak you feel will never go away—but, with faith, trust, and the ability to let go of your need for control, it can soften. It's kind of like air-brushed photographs—the essence is still there, only softened around the edges.

Although Leah Ann is still enmeshed with the day-to-day issues associated with Alzheimer's, it's easier than when Shirley was first diagnosed. She considers other residents at Applewood Our House as members of her family, and she treats them as such—not only those in her facility where she works, but at her mom's house, as well.

Somehow, it all works.

So, Shirley continues to experience her decline according to Alzheimer's, and Leah Ann sometimes thinks about how things used to be—how could she not? Not the rearview mirror, but the wonderful memories of her mom. Her favorite?

When she auditioned for All State Choir.

For those not of a musical bent, All State Choir is a serious competition for high school singers, and the audition process is not for those who don't feel like preparing. It's a huge amount of work—and, Leah Ann practiced. And, practiced. And, practiced. But, was it enough? She wondered. The competition was made of stuff sparking unexpected tears, frustration, and anxiety—all of which made Leah Ann cry. Well, one day, the competition became too much, and Leah Ann fell into her mom's arms, sobbing. "Why is she crying, again," her father asked, not considering it was a teenage girl thing.

"Just shut up, and let her cry!" Whether Shirley threw him 'the look' is unknown, but one can well imagine.

So, you see, Shirley was the wonderful mom who knew exactly what her daughter needed—she allowed Leah Ann to vent her frustrations, knowing all she needed was a little support.

The short version is weeks passed before learning the results of the choir competition, Shirley always telling her daughter how proud she was of her. Finally, the results were posted, and Leah Ann was chosen as the only alto in Jefferson County to make it.

A major deal.

Of course, such stories are hugely personal, but, Leah Ann knows those dealing with Alzheimer's will take refuge in similar special moments—the things they remember.

Memories making their hearts sing . . .

SHIRLEY DODRILL

CHAPTER TWELVE

Shirley

*I*t's said moms and daughters sometimes have a difficult time getting along, especially during teen years—the time when tempers flare, perceived injustices are points of contention, and insults such as 'you don't understand me' are uttered with alarming frequency.

Not so with Shirley Dodrill, and her daughter, Valerie.

They were best friends.

Another western gal, Shirley grew up in Englewood, Colorado, with her sister and brother—Shirley was the youngest, just like her mom, and, that's what was interesting—no one really considered Shirley wouldn't be just like her when it came to her health. Her mom was still going strong six years past the century mark, so, it was a surprise when Shirley began showing signs of deteriorating memory. Of course, there were signals—missing slippers, forgetting social engagements, and repetitive behavior. What Valerie and her family didn't realize at the time, however, was Alzheimer's was beginning to make itself known. Her symptoms were typical and common, but, unless there's familiarity, chances are good little clues can be missed. It was when Shirley began taking tissues out of the box, refolding them, then replacing them, discussions about taking her to the doctor cropped up—even then, Alzheimer's wasn't in the realm of possibility, and it didn't enter their minds.

Until the official diagnosis.

Then, denial.

"Oh, I'm just getting old," she'd say as she aged, completely negating the possibility of such an insidious disease. Finally, such comments sparked the necessity of finding a caring facility for her and, by the time they did, Shirley was deeply entrenched in dementia—Alzheimer's. In fact, her progression was so rapid, Valerie couldn't connect with her mom by the time she entered memory care, commenting to people it was like 'missing her mom while she's still here.'

So, the search for a suitable memory care facility began, Shirley needing to make certain she found the best. Unfortunately, she didn't have the luxury of taking her time—by the time Shirley was diagnosed, she couldn't comprehend a move, and needing expert care was imminent. That meant a walk-through of each facility—sometimes as many as ten on the weekend—but, before anything could be done, there was red tape.

A lot of it.

In the meantime, Valerie was in the position of caring for her mother, compounded by Randy's serious brain injury—

as well as a full-time job—and, it was a full six months before preparations morphed into reality. Valerie's brother did what he could, helping with insurance requirements, as well as other paperwork needing to be done, but it wasn't easy getting their mother's affairs in order.

It wasn't easy taking care of someone else's business . . .

Finally, the move.

Changes are never easy, and Shirley's was no different. Valerie's concerns centered around her mom's not only adjusting to her new environment, but her ability to make friends, as well—a huge factor when choosing the best residence. Touring facilities, many housed over one hundred or more residents, so, when she did a walk-through at Applewood Our House, it was a relief to learn there were options. Caring for only sixteen residents at one time, it was clear caregivers were engaged, kind, and respectful, and the 'homey vibe' Valerie noticed was much different than larger memory care facilities.

On the day she was slated to move in, Valerie and Randy were invited to stay for dinner, but Randy couldn't—the emotional upheaval was too great. Still, as much as Valerie wanted him to stay, she understood, watching him leave with tears in his eyes.

Sometime after dinner, a caregiver pulled her aside. "I think it's best—when you leave—to just go. No big goodbyes. It will be best for Shirley . . ."

"What about calling her?"

"Not for about a week—it's important she gets used to things here and, if you're calling or visiting, it will be harder to integrate into our routine."

So, that's what she did. Without fanfare, Valerie quietly left after dinner on Shirley's first day at Applewood, then sat in her car for an hour, sobbing, the guilt unbearable.

Yet, she knew it was the way it had to be.

For the first three or four weeks, everything was fine, and it was then Valerie and her husband decided to make their dream of owning a restaurant come true. Valerie talked to Shirley about it many times before Alzheimer's, her mom always excited about their possibilities. Such conversations, however, became memories for Valerie, and she and her husband knew they needed to make a change—the hard truth was Shirley most likely wouldn't know.

Based on the commitment to visit her mom on a regular basis, Valerie and her husband embarked on a discovery trip, finally deciding to relocate to southern Indiana—the perfect place for their new restaurant, new days, and new life.

Decision made, Valerie spent as much time with her mom as she could, still juggling her eighty-five hour work-week—and, for the first few months, Shirley continued to adjust. Even so, her attitude was somewhat mercurial, and she'd yell at Valerie whenever she had to leave. There was no doubt Shirley blamed her daughter for her 'situation,' not hesitating to let her know. "It's your fault," Shirley screamed and, to some degree, Valerie supposed she was right.

More guilt.

As you can imagine, one of the hardest things for Valerie was seeing the about-face change in her mom. Shirley's chameleon-like shift to someone she barely recognized was difficult to swallow, leaving her daughter to bear the brunt. In Shirley's world, nothing else made sense. In Valerie's world?

Nothing, but grief and sadness.

As weeks passed, Valerie noticed something in Shirley, fracturing her heart. It wasn't immediately noticeable because there was so much to do after the diagnosis, as well as getting her transitioned into Applewood Our House. But, once Shirley had been there awhile? There was one thing missing . . .

A smile.

Although Valerie tried, taking Shirley out and about to do things she enjoyed was quickly becoming increasingly difficult. But, when Valerie offered to take her for a drive in the mountains—jackpot! A brief smile. A second of joy.

A feeling of happiness.

Then, there was feeding geese at the park—one of Shirley's favorite things. Her broad smile and twinkling eyes filled Valerie's soul—such moments, however, were fleeting, and life as Shirley knew it resumed within minutes. Maybe, seconds. When Valerie thought about it, she wondered what it must be like for her mother—and, she couldn't imagine.

It was a burden no one should bear.

Soon, life became about memories.

Quicker than she'd like to acknowledge, life with her mom became one of recalling weekends when they played games, or figuring out puzzles they thought they'd never piece together—but, somehow, they always did.

"You know what I love most about Mom," Valerie asked her brother as they sat in the car after a visit with Shirley.

"Actually, I can think of a few things . . ."

"Well, that's true—but, what I remember most, I think, is her listening. I could talk to her about anything, and she'd listen, figuring out how she could help me."

Randy agreed. "I know what you mean . . ."

"Remember when I was trying to figure out whether I should go to cosmetology school?"

"Kind of . . ."

"When I told Mom, she was so engaged—I suppose I should have known what I wanted to do after high school, but I didn't. When we talked about it, she went over all of the pros and cons, walking me through making a decision by—and, for—myself."

"That sounds like her!"

"And, not once did she tell me what I should do . . ."

"She did that with me, too," Randy laughed, "although, I never really thought about it . . ."

"You know, though—I think Mom knew I'd never go to cosmetology school. She knew I had more in me—not that there's anything bad about cosmetology—but, when I was accepted to play college basketball, she must have had a feeling of satisfaction . . ."

"She knew . . ."

So, there Valerie and her brother sat, memories of Shirley filling their conversation . . .

And, hearts.

Throughout the course of Shirley's illness, when Valerie mentioned to friends her mom was in memory care, there were questions. The fact Alzheimer's and dementia affect people differently, Shirley didn't really go through the stage of being repetitive—in fact, when they first suspected something was amiss, they didn't consider Alzheimer's because of repetitive behavior—it was her increasing forgetfullness. Shirley could tell her a story about something and, thirty minutes later, her mom wouldn't remember a bit of it.

A giant red flag.

Even so, they didn't act on Nature's warning. "Well, I guess if we did . . ." Valerie surmised, "maybe things would have been different." But, the truth?

Probably not.

It's thoughts such as those sparking conversations about the necessity of catching it early. "If someone thinks there's an issue," Valerie advises, "the best thing is to get a doctor's diagnosis . . ."

Her comment is an oft spoken, familiar refrain when it comes to Alzheimer's and dementia—and, advice that shouldn't go unheeded. Why? Well, there's more than one good reason, but, mainly because the person suffering with the disease can begin medical treatment sooner, as well as qualified memory care. As much as family members may want to care for their loved one, there's little doubt doing so would be a difficult road—perhaps one impossible to navigate.

"When things started going on with Mom," Valerie confided to her colleague at work, "my family closed—functionally, I mean. I can't imagine what it would be like to deal with it for five, or ten years!"

Indeed—another comment most likely uttered more than once by friends and family of Alzheimer's and dementia patients.

The truth is it's an unrelenting disease slowly robbing people of their memories. Their lives. Clearly, things would be a whole lot easier if there were a definitive time frame—but, there isn't. Once diagnosed, patients experience dissimilar progressions— one may deal with it for a year, while others slowly sink into a world they don't recognize, lasting for fifteen years.

No one can predict.

Or, know.

"One thing I do know, however," Valerie continued, "is no matter how much the disease strips Mom of her memory, it's important to remember it's not about me. Or, my brother—it's about Mom. And, it always will be about her . . ."

So, as Valerie continued to move through stages of loving an Alzheimer's patient, she realized there wasn't much she could do to help care for her mom. After moving to southern Indiana, she realized she didn't have to be with Shirley every moment of every day—visiting every two months, and calls on holidays eased the pain, but probably more for Valerie than her mom. Although, to be honest, chances were pretty good Shirley wouldn't remember. Still, it was important Valerie maintain her connection, perhaps considering it the least she could do to repay her mom for all the things she did for her daughter—whether Shirley remembered, or not.

As the illness progressed, frequent visits enriched Valerie's life, and she knew it helped Shirley's, as well. It was good for them to interact during all stages of the disease, although it did get more difficult as the Alzheimer's dug in with unrelenting tenacity. Accompanied by a series of small strokes, there was obvious cognitive damage—but, for the most part, it wasn't noticeable. Those who knew her chalked it up to Shirley's having a bad day, or being tired—at least, that's what they said.

No one really considered something as serious as vascular dementia.

CHAPTER THIRTEEN

Honoring Memories

*M*onths passed.

Shirley continued to decline and, on May 21, 2019, Shirley Dodrill fought her last battle with Alzheimer's and vascular dementia.

Everyone at Applewood gathered to say their goodbyes, caregivers as teary-eyed as family. One put her arm around Valerie, giving her a gentle squeeze. "Your mom was so thug," she told her, although Valerie wasn't quite sure what she meant.

"You know—strong! Tough! Ready to take on anyone!"

"I'll miss talking to her everyday . . ."

"Of course, you will—but, you were with her, and that's so important."

True. Valerie was with Shirley for the four days leading to her passing, holding her hand—yet, she was angry. Angry at God. "Why does there have to be so much pain and suffering with passing," she asked herself more than once.

Watching her mother struggle to hang on was almost more than she could bear. Before Shirley passed, the hospice nurse called via FaceTime, providing Valerie an opportunity to show her mom the new restaurant. Shirley couldn't speak, but she smiled, her mouth open in awe, and Valerie knew her mom was proud of her daughter.

Four hours later, the hospice nurse called again, informing Valerie her mom was unresponsive.

Valerie was on the first flight to Colorado.

She stayed with her day and night, sleeping on a mattress on the floor of Shirley's room, not wanting her mom to be alone. On the first day of her arrival, Shirley couldn't form words, but had eye contact and expressions.

The second day, she was experiencing pain while laying on one side, unresponsive. Valerie stroked her hair, then played her favorite songs—Neil Diamond, and a hymn, "In the Garden."

Day three—tears. "You'll always be in my heart," Valerie told her. "It's okay to go . . ."

After a peaceful night, the following morning Valerie awakened, noticing her mom's breathing changed. She watched as her body relaxed, her face soften, and, finally, her breathing stopped. For ten minutes Valerie sat with her, an unrelenting grief gripping her soul.

Those private moments with her mom etched in memory, Valerie contacted caregivers, and calls were made. Soon, people were saying goodbye in ways only they could.

Interestingly, Shirley knew who Valerie was for those four, gut-wrenching, soul-filled days. Although Valerie did most of the talking, together they recalled the 'high school prom' Shirley attended shortly before her passing.

It was really quite the soirée—most residents from the Applewood Our House homes got gussied up, high school girls applying their makeup with master precision.

Providing wonderful memories for her family, Shirley wore one of her favorite blouses, and she laughed as she danced the night away.

Well, at least until seven o'clock.

The festive mood lasted until they returned to Applewood—but, not for long. By the time they crawled into bed that evening, most had already forgotten.

Including Shirley.

Days later, after the services, Valerie couldn't help but reflect on the previous six years. Although her heart ached with sorrow, she knew one thing. She would talk to her mom every day . . .

Honoring her memory.

LARRY BOYE

CHAPTER FOURTEEN

LARRY

*S*ome say music comes from the soul—if that's true, Larry Boye was living proof. From the time he was old enough to tie his own shoes, he was a song and dance man, and nobody was going to hold him back from what he knew he was born to do.

For most of his early life, Larry lived in a town that curls up its sidewalks before dark and, growing up, life wasn't easy. An early death claiming his mom, his father struggled with alcohol, and Larry was eventually shipped off to live with his cousins until it came time to think about college.

Finally, with a dream of teaching music tucked under his arm, he entered Bethany College and, later, Wichita State, earning bachelor's and master's degrees in music education. But, while academics got him where he needed to be, his heart was never far from the stage. Until he graduated, he spent summers performing in multiple musicals at the Starlight Theater in Wichita, Kansas—then, his high school teaching career took root.

And, what a career it was!

Soon out of college, Larry met the girl who would capture his heart and they married, children gracing their lives not long after—a daughter of their own, and a boy they adopted and loved as if he'd been with them forever. It was no secret—J.D. and Tammy stole his heart, too.

Teaching high school in Hoxie and Columbus, Kansas, he soon changed trajectory to direct choral groups and musicals at Manhattan High School, including the Manhattan Pops Choir. Yet, that's not all—from a tiny town, Larry Boye rose to prominence as Director of the Ball State University Singers in Indiana from 1968 to 1985. Performing in dozens of states and countries around the world—including presidential inaugurations, and USO tours—Larry and his singers spread goodwill through music to the point the group was designated Goodwill Ambassadors of the State of Indiana.

Wow!

Now, you might think that was the end of it—but, as you know, things change. After leaving Ball State, Larry continued his career as a vocal specialist for Walt Disney Productions before returning to teaching at Brevard Community College in Florida in 1987. There, he directed musicals as well as several choral groups that also performed worldwide.

Still, he wasn't done. Finally, he rounded out his career as a consultant for The Young Americans College of the Performing Arts in Los Angeles, once more traveling to many states and countries, encouraging hundreds of students in their performance careers. Landing in Colorado and a prominent force in the Young American's group, he finally decided to retire in 2009.

Yes, indeed—music dripped from Larry Boye's soul.

But, life wasn't sweet music for Larry and his wife. After many years together, tiny fractures in their marriage began to appear, and, finally, they decided to go their separate ways. Interestingly, the split provided a bit of freedom for Larry's kids to watch him in action, filling their memory banks as he worked for Disney. J.D. particularly enjoyed when college kids visited so they could study with Larry, and there was never a shortage of enthusiasm and talent.

It was when J.D. learned to drive he formed true appreciation for his father's career, heading to performance locations to watch rehearsals—and, it was also around that time he was dealing with raw emotions of his parents' divorce. As a senior in high school, it was clear they had issues, and it wasn't long before the person who would become Larry's second wife drifted into the picture.

Life again morphing for Larry, he and his second wife moved to Florida while J.D. and Tammy flew the nest for college—a time when they were somewhat estranged from their dad. For Tammy, it was a particularly troublesome time in her life for she recalled enjoying when she and Larry would sing duets, or sing together in church. There was no doubt they had a deep connection—so, when Larry picked up stakes, she, too, felt her heart fracture.

Shortly after graduating from college, J.D. relocated to Colorado, married and had kids, and Tammy went her way, only to return to the mountain state years later. Eventually, Larry and his wife, too, moved west where Larry continued working with high school and college groups, always focused on improving their performing chops. J.D. often wondered if his father's commitment to music caused rifts between his mom and dad—if so, would the same thing happen?

The answer would only come with time.

J.D.'s concerns, however, were cast aside, and life in Colorado was good until about 2009—that's when little clues about Larry's compromised memory began to surface. As with many Alzheimer's and dementia patients, the progression wasn't swift, and they didn't give it serious thought until they realized Larry Boye was fading into a space where he'd no longer recall his remarkable life.

Or, his children.

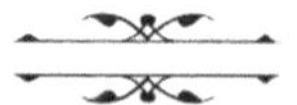

That's when things started to get . . . uncomfortable.

Larry was always a church-going man, but, when he started to forget names and faces, his friends and family realized things weren't quite right. Of course, he made a valiant effort to cover it up by making a joke—still, when he didn't recognize one of his favorite people, those close to him knew something was up. Another clue? Larry was giving away money—not to people he knew, but to scam artists, and those who didn't care whom they swindled.

Even so, Larry was a very lucky man—his bank recognized inconsistencies, and his daughter was beginning to notice her dad's mentioning how he was going to get a bunch of money—and, that's when J.D., decided to investigate. Luckily, it didn't take him long to figure out Larry was getting rooked, and knowing someone was swindling him was more than infuriating. So, with his sister's blessing, J.D. took responsibility of his dad's finances.

How the bank figured out something was amiss was a little trickier—someone within its ranks noticed money was leaking from Larry's account, much of it going to suspicious organizations. A call to the Arvada, Colorado, police department later, a senior liaison got involved, ultimately figuring out what was happening. Finally working through it, there was one thing J.D. and Tammy knew . . .

Time was taking its toll.

In 2011, Larry's behavior was such J.D. and Tammy had the difficult conversation to discuss their dad's living circumstances. "He'll fight it all the way, you know," Tammy commented.

"That may be—but, he can't drive anymore, and the fact is we need to have him tested for Alzheimer's. And, if it's not that, it might be something similar . . ."

Tammy was quiet, her brother's words stinging her heart. She knew he was right—Larry's continuing to drive was an issue. Yet, when J.D. suggested taking their father's car away, it seemed such a punitive measure for only a few dents and dings—which Larry couldn't recall how they happened.

Eyes brimming with tears, she finally agreed . . .

It was time.

For some reason, we often tend to put things off—important things. Things we know need attention. Things we don't want entering our minds. Yet, such niggling thoughts never seem to disappear, and it's only when we take action, things change.

So it was for J.D. and Tammy.

Even without an official diagnosis, both still considered the idea of moving their dad into some sort of assisted living. After all, he still had his car, and they weren't quite ready to think about putting him into memory care. In many ways, the truth was Larry was still capable of independent living—they suspected however, he would continue to decline, and transitioning to assisted living seemed a good move to middle ground until the time came when Larry's condition would progress.

After many discussions, both finally agreed, and Larry moved into an independent living facility for about a year—and, in 2013, the time came to make another adjustment by finally taking his car away.

He wasn't happy.

Eventually, however, he began to forget about his car and, not long after, he didn't bring it up again. The few times he did, memories were skewed, barely representing the true situation.

As a result—and, not unexpectedly—the 'A' word began to creep into his children's conversations frequently, and both knew it was time for assisted living. At that time, Larry's regular physician wasn't specialized in memory deficiency, and J.D. and Tammy felt the necessity to seek a doctor who could help—one specializing in Alzheimer's.

In the fall of 2014, it was official.

Shortly thereafter, J.D. took Larry out to eat, and it was then the realization of his father's illness took root. After a few bites, Larry looked at J.D., fork poised, then asked a question which clearly was bothering him. "What's your name, again?"

An unintentional stab to the heart.

CHAPTER FIFTEEN

TIME BANDIT

Decision made.

In 2015, J.D. and Tammy arranged to transition their dad into one of the Applewood Our House homes, unsure of how he would adjust. "What do you think he'll miss most," Tammy asked her brother shortly after Larry's move.

"I don't know—it's hard to say. But, I'm willing to bet it won't take him long to play the piano . . ."

J.D. was right.

For Applewood residents, it was wonderful Larry was such a showman—whenever he played, his fingers danced on the keys, filling the room with show tunes everyone recognized. Smiles were plentiful, and there was no question his music filled their souls, too. Caregivers, as well, made it a point to listen for a minute or two, a few caught singing as they went about their business.

Soon after, time and change became inextricably linked as Larry began to show definitive signs of Alzheimer's—an increasing downward spiral, leaving his family to think more about time. How to make the best of it.

How much was left.

As the disease progressed, J.D. and Tammy grew to accept their father's condition. Although, Tammy was more reluctant to express understanding that her father would not remember her as he acquiesced to the illness's final stages.

For J.D., acceptance resulted from taking care of Larry's daily business. More embroiled in the day-to-day, watching his dad's deterioration from a one-on-one vantage point allowed him to slowly accept the ultimate. Did that mean he was more prepared for Alzheimer's eventuality?

Probably not.

While J.D. took care of finances, Tammy turned her attention to the medical aspects of Larry's illness—but, it was tough. Trying to semi-retire, dealing with her dad's Alzheimer's was taking its toll, and she finally made the decision to move to South Carolina for a year and a half—maybe, two years. It was during that time Larry began to experience additional health issues, the more serious being chronic heart failure—or, at least, the beginning of it. Circulation and heart issues finally earned him a trip to the hospital.

Everything seemed to be happening at once.

But, that wasn't all—in 2016, Larry took a tumble, resulting in surgery to repair his leg. After that? Two or three months of rehab. The short story is he never was quite the same—walking was trying, really, and all he could do was stand. Piano? Not so much.

A difficult thing for a song and dance man.

As Larry recovered, J.D. learned everything depended on logistics. He lived east of the metro, and Larry was in rehab west of the metro—travel time took planning. Adding to his stress was knowledge the rehab facility didn't cater to Alzheimer's—risk of rolling out of bed was considerable, as was standing. And, it wasn't only once or twice a week—multiple trips to check on Larry made the situation more tedious, and time-consuming.

Even so, he was willing to do anything for his dad.

Finally, Larry received the go-ahead to take advantage of the rehab facility's assisted living program, which made things a little easier while he continued to recover—if nothing else, it eased J.D.'s mind because of the available care. Wheelchair bound, Larry was no longer mobile, but J.D. suspected it wasn't because of his leg injury. To him, it made more sense his dad simply forgot how to walk—or, that he could walk.

He wasn't sure which.

As helpful as the assisted living facility at the rehab center was, there was still the issue of its not being prepared for Alzheimer's patients—and, to return to Applewood Our House required Larry's ability to get in and out of his wheelchair by himself. Clearly, that was going to take time.

J.D. realized the best thing for his father was to get him back at Applewood, and the opportunity presented itself when rehab caregivers caught Larry wandering in and out of other residents' room.

"We just can't have that," the facility spokesperson told J.D.

"But, Applewood . . ."

"I know—I'm sorry, but you'll need to make other arrangements."

The news was a blow, but J.D. figured it was worth one more try—he knew Applewood was the best place for his dad.

Unfortunately, there was little Applewood could offer, or do. "The reason we can't take him is because of the wheelchair requirement," Sherrie told him. "We don't have the people—or, the lift—to legally place him with us."

That meant another rehab facility.

Just west of the first rehab place, it didn't make J.D.'s commute less stressful. On a good day, visiting his dad could take at least an hour each way.

Again, J.D. didn't mind.

It was during one of his many visits, the rehab's client-care coordinator delivered the news. "Your dad isn't participating, anymore . . ."

J.D. didn't need to ask questions—he knew exactly what her words implied. "So, it's back to assisted living . . ."

"I'm afraid so . . ."

By the time all decision-making conversations came to an end, they had a plan. One facility they located offered hospice evaluation, as well as weekly or biweekly nursing visits to monitor Larry's progress. There was no mistake—as soon as Larry could get in and out of his wheelchair by himself, he would be out of there, on his way back to Applewood.

And, that's exactly what happened.

Close to his birthday in February, 2017, his second transition to Applewood took place, and Applewood chipped in a little extra care, but not to the point of having someone help Larry in and out of his chair. After all, he was still strong, and tipped in at about two hundred pounds. How did Larry handle it?

He refused to get out of bed.

Back to rehab.

Then, back to Applewood. From then on, Larry could get in and out of his wheelchair, meeting all of Applewood's legal requirements. So, as 2017 rounded toward summer, things were going pretty well.

Well—as well as could be expected.

Tammy returned to Colorado about that time, taking some of the emotional stress from her brother. A much appreciated gesture, J.D. could finally relax, but, he found his emotions were somewhat in check. He surmised it was due to having to take care of the logistics of Larry's illness and, without realizing, doing so kept him on an even keel. Still, the fact Larry was back at Applewood, and his sister's help?

J.D. could take a breather.

He didn't visit as often, fully aware at Larry's stage of Alzheimer's, visits were more for him than his dad. The sad fact was Larry didn't remember him and, most likely, had no expectation of visits. By the end of 2017, it had been a good couple of years since Larry recognized his son, even though there were flickers of memory.

Brief, and short-lived.

CHAPTER SIXTEEN

FINAL BOW

Applewood and Larry's hospice nurse always kept J.D. apprised of his dad's condition via weekly emails, and the time finally arrived when they informed him Larry's condition progressed to the next stage of Alzheimer's. The hospice nurse also mentioned it was the stage during which most of her patients passed.

Larry, however, was having none of it.

Then, months later, the time came—the call they didn't want to get. "It can be days, or a week, or two," the hospice nursed told J.D.

He was quiet, the realization of his dad's imminent passing settling on his heart. " But, we . . . my family . . . we have a trip planned." Little did he know when he uttered those words, he'd beat himself up about them for months to come.

J.D. saw his father for the last time the night before they left. He never talked to his wife about his decision—if he did, he probably would have changed his mind, or found his way home after their departure. He did talk to his sister, though, never expressing he wouldn't be there with her.

That was on a Friday. On Monday, the hospice nurse sent an email letting J.D. know Larry's passing was within a couple of days.

There's no doubt his was a difficult decision to make—with it, however, came a sweet irony. Their trip? Florida. Disney. Shows.

All the things his dad loved.

They flew home to Colorado on Saturday, February 20, 2018. Larry passed on Friday, February 19, 2018 . . .

His final bow.

CHAPTER SEVENTEEN

TOUCHING LIVES

The passing of someone greatly loved is always difficult and, as soon as J.D. returned from Florida, it was time to think about funeral arrangements—it would be a time when family learned of love, and appreciation.

Although few attended Larry's funeral in Denver, Kansas was a different story. Two of his former students attended it and the burial, one gentlemen arriving from San Francisco. And, judging by comments and tributes on social media, there was no question Larry Boye touched lives. Social media exploded with conversations and memories zipping back and forth, each recalling special moments when Larry made dreams come true.

Of course, there were several questions during private conversations—some asked what were the most difficult things Larry and his family endured after Larry was diagnosed. Perhaps they asked out of concern—or, perhaps, they were in the same position. Either way, J.D.'s answer was the same. "Transition—there was always a sense of the unknown. At least until we got Dad into Applewood—before then, he was independent for a while, but, after the diagnosis, we had him in assisted living, rehab, you name it . . . but, Applewood was where we really needed him to be."

"It sounds as if it's where *he* needed to be . . ." One of Larry's former students voice softened, as if in a place of reverence.

"There's always going to be stress," J.D. continued, "but, when we didn't have to worry as much . . ."

She nodded. "I know what you mean—I'm going through the same thing with my mom."

J.D. didn't quite know what to say. "I'm not going to lie—you're going to have moments when you think you can't handle the stress, anymore. That's when I had to step back, and reorient my thinking—my emotions, too."

Larry's student's eyes welled with tears. "We're just in the beginning stages as of last month. That's when we got the official diagnosis . . ."

J.D. put his arm around her shoulders, "If there's anything I can tell you, it's this—plan as best you can, get done what you have to do, and allow yourself to grieve. Not only down the road, but, now, as well . . ."

"I can't help thinking about what I'm going to miss—and, I know that sounds selfish."

"Not at all—in fact, I felt the same way. Even now, there are things I miss, and it's only been a week."

A sniffle. "Like what?"

"Well—I've been searching for someone who has a recording of his singing."

"He had such an incredible voice!"

J.D. smiled. "Yes, he did—I wish I could still hear it."

"I'm sure you will . . ." With that, she gave J.D. a gentle hug filled with understanding, then disappeared through the funeral home door, a tissue in her hand at the ready.

Good luck, J.D. thought as he watched her go. *Good luck* . . .

As he turned to greet other guests, he suddenly thought of one thing he forgot to tell her. Just then, his wife linked her arm through his. "Who was that," she asked.

"An old student of Dad's—she just found out her mom has Alzheimer's.

"Oh, no! Well, at least you could give her a little advice . . ."

"Maybe—but, I forgot to tell her one of the most important things . . ."

She turned to look at him, noticing tears in his eyes. "And, that is . . ."

"Telling your loved one you love them—you know, how you feel about them, and how they make you feel. But, tell them when they can still understand. That's what's really important . . ."

Gently, she took his hand in hers. "Life is all about touching lives—and, your dad did that in spades!"

Loving her more in that moment, he grinned. "He sure as hell did! And, I'll bet money he's still singing!"

Together, they stepped outside onto the sidewalk in front of the funeral home, enjoying the faint warmth of a winter sun.

"I was lucky to have him . . ."

"And, he was lucky to have you!" She paused, thinking. "Two lives touched . . ."

A tear slipped down J.D.'s cheek. "They always will . . ."

When I graduated from college with a B.A. in The Study of Theatre Education, I thought teaching students how to perform was how I'd spend my days—photography, too. Both are passions, filling my soul, and I felt great about my life's path.

Well—things changed.

When I first had the opportunity to meet one of the residents at an Applewood Our House home, I knew I had to photograph her and others, never, of course, considering how that photo would change my life's trajectory. After the photo sessions, it was then I knew I needed to write a book honoring the six individuals introduced to you in *About Faces: Expressions of Alzheimer's and Dementia.*

How to go about doing it was the trick.

So, the idea simmered on my mind's back burner until someone from my past got in touch with me for a reason I can't recall. "How are things going in your life," I asked, never expecting her response.

"Well, I retired from teaching, and I'm a writer and book editor . . ."

I was stunned. "Really? Congrats on your retirement—and, it so happens I'm looking for an editor!"

So, you can imagine the conversation . . .

By the following day, my manuscript and ideas were in her hands, and *About Faces: Expressions of Alzheimer's* became a reality.

As we waded through my writing, one thing became clear—my book wasn't about Alzheimer's, it's symptoms, and what to do about it. No—I realized it was about something else. Something equally important.

Emotion.

During the neophyte stages of the book, I conducted interviews—more like intimate, personal conversations, really—with the family members of the Applewood Our House residents I photographed. Willing to share their experiences with the thought of helping others, each confided their memories—the ups. Downs. Everything in-between. At times, I wondered if I were intruding as I teared up with them, hoping I could do their thoughts and feelings justice. Honestly?

I wasn't sure I could pull it off.

My new editor, however, knew I could. "I'm not saying it will be easy," she told me when she reviewed the manuscript. "It'll take a little polishing—but, these are stories that must be told."

So, that was it. We were off and running in a direction I didn't know I was going until that day in November, 2016, when I photographed Eileen Tinker. Alzheimer's and dementia, I learned, wasn't simply a devastating diagnosis—it signaled a change in everything familiar.

If there were a rule book on how to shoulder the grief and eventual acceptance, things would be easier, I suppose—but, even if there were one, I'm not sure it would do much good. As much as all of us can learn about the physical and mental challenges of the disease, there are few willing to talk about the roller coaster of emotions streaking out of control without a clue of how to stop, and get off.

Sitting down to write was easy—getting words on the page was the tough part. As I thought about each person interviewed, I realized I spoke with only six individuals who entered difficult times in their lives. But, as I caught a glimpse of someone walking down the sidewalk outside of my window, I was struck by the understanding everyone goes through something. That guy who just passed me without knowing it? Who knows what his life is like? Or, what celebrations—or, tragedies—he has notched on his belt?

Everyone, I realized, has an unexpected truth.

So, there I sat, staring at my laptop, when, suddenly, I knew which direction I needed to go. *If I write this as some sort of medical treatise*, I thought, *no one will know the real story . . .* Once I decided I wanted to help those going through the same thing by talking about emotions, I knew what I was meant to say. I wanted to provide an outlet where someone might recognize their situation. Their stories. Themselves.

I needed them to know tears, frustration, and indecision are okay.

I hope *About Faces: Expressions of Alzheimer's and Dementia* helps . . .

Taylor Hulett

ACKNOWLEDGMENTS

To my beautiful, amazingly supportive wife, Anna—thank you.

To my incredible family and friends for all of their support.

A huge thank you to Barbara Stewart—without her, this book would still be just an idea.

To the incredible L.A. O'Neil, my editor, for her insight, skills, and knowledge—they're irreplaceable. Also, many thanks to Wyatt Ilsley at High Mountain Design for his stunning cover design.

To the amazing team at Applewood Our House—the love and care shown by each and every caregiver, leadership team member, and family member is astonishing.

Finally, thank you to the caregivers—in memory care, or in any capacity—the love and care you provide is essential, and absolutely amazing!

PROFESSIONAL ACKNOWLEDGMENTS

CHRYSALIS PUBLISHING AUTHOR SERVICES
L.A. O'NEIL, Editor
www.chrysalis-pub.com
chrysalispub@gmail.com

HIGH MOUNTAIN DESIGN
WYATT ILSLEY, Cover design
www.highmountaindesign.com
hmdesign89@gmail.com

TAYLOR HULETT PHOTOGRAPHY
TAYLOR HULETT, Photos, Cover Design
www.taylorhulettphotography.com
taylorvanhulett@gmail.com